# VICTORIAN
# HOUSE STYLE
## *Handbook*

A DAVID & CHARLES BOOK
Copyright © David & Charles Limited 2007

David & Charles is an F+W Publications Inc. company
4700 East Galbraith Road
Cincinnati, OH 45236

First published in 1991 as *Victorian House Style*
This revised edition first published in 2007

Original edition first published in 1991 as *Victorian House
Style* and conceived, edited and designed by John Strange
and Megra Mitchell
Researchers: Chris Gomes, Charlotte Osborne

Illustrations copyright © John Strange 1991, 2001, 2007
Text copyright © Linda Osband 1991, 2001, 2007

A catalogue record for this book is available from the
British Library.

ISBN-13: 978-0-7153-2705-0 paperback
ISBN-10: 0-7153-2705-4 paperback

Printed in China by Shenzen R R Donnelly Printing Co Ltd
for David & Charles
Brunel House, Newton Abbot, Devon

Commissioning Editor: Jane Trollope
Assistant Editor: Louise Clark
Senior Designer: Sarah Clark
Copy Editor: Wendy Toole
Production Controller: Ros Napper

Visit our website at www.davidandcharles.co.uk

David & Charles books are available from all good
bookshops; alternatively you can contact our Orderline
on 0870 9908222 or write to us at FREEPOST EX2 110,
D&C Direct, Newton Abbot, TQ12 4ZZ (no stamp require
UK only); US customers call 800-289-0963 and Canadian
customers call 800-840-5220.

# VICTORIAN HOUSE STYLE
## *Handbook*

LINDA OSBAND
**EDITED BY PAUL ATTERBURY**

David and Charles

# Contents

# Foreword

*Architect: 'You choose the style of your house just as you choose the build of your hat; – you can have classical, either columnar or non-columnar, either arcuated or trabeated, either rural or civil, or indeed palatial; you can have Elizabethan in equal variety; Renaissance ditto; or ... Mediaeval – the Gothic which is now so much the rage – in any one of its multifarious forms ... feudalistic, monastic, scholastic, ecclesiastic, archaeologistic, ecclesiologistic, and so on.' Gentleman Client: 'But really, I would much rather not. I want a plain, substantial, comfortable Gentleman's House ... I don't want any style at all.'*

Robert Kerr, *The Gentleman's House* (1864)

The Victorian age was the most dynamic, inventive and enterprising in British history. At the same time it is the most confusing for people with twenty-first century attitudes. The legacy of the Victorians is all around us, in technology, science and engineering, in our attitudes to travel and the global experience, in our dependence upon communication and even in our concepts of time and space. However, for most of us, the greatest and the most immediate Victorian experience is the house. Victorian buildings are in every city, town and village in Britain and most of us have lived in them at one time or another. After all, it was the Victorians who invented the modern family house and they built them in their hundreds of thousands, in terraces, detached and semi-detached and in suburban estates. Many still form the bulk of Britain's housing stock and in general they are practical, efficient and comfortable. As a result, many people happily choose to live in Victorian buildings but they do want them to be modern and to work well, while retaining their particular Victorian quality. This book will help you to achieve that balance between authenticity and practical modernity.

The Victorians invented universal and accessible interior design and they were great stylists. Their ideas came from many sources. A sense of history brought them Gothic, Classical, Renaissance. Their love of exoticism and the Imperial experience brought them China, Japan, India, the Middle East and South America. Their love of nature gave them a wealth of decorative design ideas. At the end of their century, an increasing enthusiasm for modernism brought new ideas of simplicity.

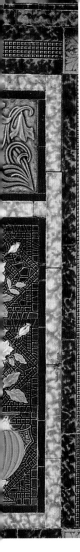

**Previous page:** The Gothic Revival movement was one of the many architectural styles battling for prominence in the mid-Victorian era, Its influence can be seen on this house in north London built in 1865.

**Far left:** With the mass production of wall tiles from the 1870s, flowered picture tiles soon adorned the porch entrances of even simple terraced houses.

**Left:** Reflecting the taste for simpler styles later in the century, one design manual of 1894 gave advice on how to convert the no-longer fashionable rosewood chiffonier into a small drawing-room bookcase.

**Below:** Classical forms and floral designs were the predominant decorative motifs during the nineteenth century.

The Victorians could have all this because their technology, and their dominance of global trade, made it all possible. Tiles, wallpapers, applied decorations, fireplaces, furniture, tablewares, domestic metalwork, kitchens and bathrooms, paint and surface finishes, lighting and heating, all were made accessible through technology. Their other great enthusiasm was colour. Despite common beliefs to the contrary, the Victorians lived in an immensely colourful world. They developed artificial dyes, colour printing and mechanical methods of decorating with colour. They drew extensively upon the colours of other ages and other cultures. They filled their gardens with colourful exotic plant species. They loved colour, and the richness of the world that colour represented. In our minimal age, colour represents the greatest challenge. They also had the benefit of modern marketing techniques: mail-order catalogues, magazines, advertisements, style guides, exhibitions, all were part of the Victorian experience, along with the department store.

In the end, the greatest Victorian achievement, and the greatest Victorian legacy, is the concept of consumer choice. We can all choose how our houses look, and we can vary that choice infinitely. The restoration of a Victorian house is always a challenge, and throughout much of the twentieth century, terrible mistakes were made. Thousands of Victorian houses were devastated by insensitive restoration and modernisation, mainly because we simply did not grasp what the Victorians were all about. Today, though they seem further away, we do understand them better and we do appreciate that they were the makers of our modern world, whether we like it or not. Getting restoration right is

**All:** These highly ornate pieces of furniture and accessories epitomise the over-decorated High Victorian style on show at the Great Exhibition. In reaction, the leaders of the Arts and Crafts movement turned back to nature and to simple, traditional craftsmanship for their inspiration.

not a tedious struggle with inconvenient authenticity, but a process of making the best of a house that was probably designed initially with comfort in mind. There is no need for slavish adherence to the past. To respond to the needs of an old house, and get it right within the bounds of modern practicality is a great achievement and a lasting pleasure. So much is in the detail, and to get that right, you need this book. It is a book about ideas and inspiration, a guide to take with you when trawling through salvage yards and to refer to when looking through the catalogues of modern manufacturers. Everything the Victorian house needs is out there somewhere, but you do need to know what you are looking for. Above all else, reading this will make the process of restoration seem an exciting challenge rather than a tedious chore.

Paul Atterbury

**All:** A selection of products on display at the Great Exhibition. Many of these highly decorated pieces of furniture found their way into the homes of the new monied middle classes, including the 'sociable' pair of mahogany or walnut chairs and the newly invented gas chandelier

# Chapter 1
# The Plan and Façade

*'However small and compact the house may be, the family must have privacy and the servants commodiousness; and the whole dwelling must display an unassuming grace. If, on the other hand, the circumstances of the owner and his tastes are such that magnitude and refinement ought to expand into state, even grandeur must not be pretentious, or wealth ostentatious, and the attributes of an agreeable English home must never be sacrificed ... They form, taken as a whole, the test of a Gentleman's House: Privacy, Comfort, Convenience, Spaciousness, Compactness, Light and Air, Salubrity, Aspect and Prospect, Cheerfulness, Elegance, Importance, Ornament.'*

Robert Kerr, *The Gentleman's House* (1864)

**Previous page:** With the rapid growth of the suburbs, streets of terraced houses such as this soon sprang up throughout the country.

Examples of different styles of detached Victorian villas.

**Below:** A house in Yorkshire designed by G. Dean in the Old English style, c. 1860.

**Centre:** The side-elevation of an Elizabethan-style house.

**Opposite:** An American clapboard seaside cottage, c. 1880.

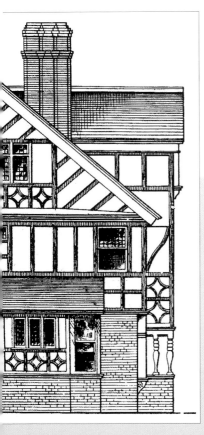

**Opposite top:** A 'middle-class' cottage designed by Norman Shaw in 1878.

**Opposite bottom:** Architect William Burgess's medieval style house in Kensington, c. 1870.

**Below:** The Red House, designed by Phillip Webb for William Morris in 1859.

Simple carved gables and decorative red brickwork
enliven an otherwise plain grey-stone façade.

**Above:** Holly Village in north London, a Gothic Revival estate built in 1865 by Baroness Burdett-Coutts for her retired servants. The architect was Henry Astley Darbishire.

**Left:** Single-storey bay windows and porches framed by simple columns with moulded capitals were typical features of many early Victorian terraces.

An American
Victorian clapboard
house, painted in a
traditional pale colour
scheme.

A row of Queen Anne Revival houses, incorporating all the elements of this architectural style: Dutch gables, tall chimneys, bay windows and warm red bricks decorated with white stonework.

The perfect layout for a row of London houses, as advocated by Robert Kerr in his book, *The Gentleman's House*, 1864.

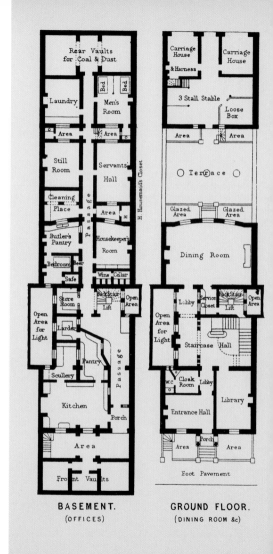

**BASEMENT.**
(OFFICES)

**GROUND FLOOR.**
(DINING ROOM &c)

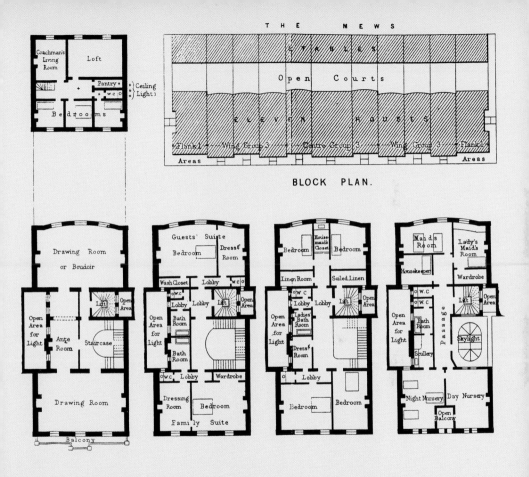

**THE  MEWS**

STABLES

Open Courts

ELEVEN HOUSES

Flank 1 — Wing Group 3 — Centre Group 3 — Wing Group 3 — Flank 1

Areas                                                                Areas

**BLOCK PLAN.**

Coachman's Living Room | Loft

Pantry ⌐ Ceiling Lights

w.c.

Bedrooms

Drawing Room or Boudoir

Open Area for Light | Ante Room | Staircase | Lift | Open Area

Drawing Room

Balcony

**FIRST FLOOR.**
(DRAWING ROOMS)

Guests' Suite

Bedroom | Dressg Room

Wash Closet | Lobby | w.c

w.c | Lobby | Lobby | Lift | Open Area

Open Area for Light | Bath Room

Bath Room

w.c | Lobby | Wardrobe

Dressing Room | Bedroom

Family Suite

**SECOND FLOOR.**
(CHIEF BEDROOMS)

Bedroom | Housemaids Closet | Bedroom

Linen Room | Soiled Linen

w.c | Ladies Bath Room

Open Area for Light | Lobby | Lobby | Lift | Open Area

Dressg Room

o | Lobby

Bedroom | Bedroom

**THIRD FLOOR.**
(SECONDARY BEDROOMS)

Maids Room | Lady's Maid's Room

Housekeeper | Wardrobe

w.c | Lift | Open Area

w.c

Open Area for Light | Bath Room | Passage | Skylight

Scullery

Night Nursery | Day Nursery

Open Balcony

**FOURTH FLOOR.**
(NURSERIES &
SERVANTS' ROOMS)

From the 1870s Americans rejected neutral colour schemes and painted their clapboard houses in bold, imaginative tones.

One of the predominant forms of town dwelling was the terrace house.

**Top:** The upper storeys of the house, where the servants' and children's quarters were. had smaller windows and little external decoration.

**Bottom:** An elegant row of brick terraced houses embellished with white stonework decoration and ornate railings bordering the front steps.

**Opposite top:** A row of Gothic villas, c. 1880.

**Above:** One of London's elegant stucco-fronted streets, with glazed porches supported by decorative ironwork.

**Opposite bottom:** A late Georgian terrace, a style still popular until the 1850s.

At the beginning of the Victorian era, the roofs of houses tended to be hidden from street vire by parapet walls, which gave an appearance of elegant uniformity to a row of terraced houses. As soon as roofs became visible in the middle of the nineteenth century, every part of them was ripe for embellishment.

**Right:** the façade of this house is decorated with overlapping fish-scale tiles and it has a balcony inset into its gable.

**Opposite:** Carved gables and mulit-shaped chimneys.

**Top:** Roof crests became fashionable on buildings from the 1880s, made either of tiles or iron.

**Opposite bottom and right:** Decorative ridge tiles and ironwork finials.

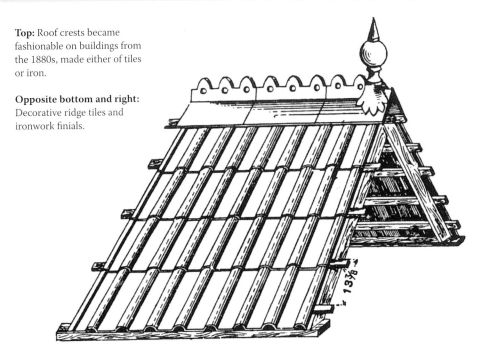

1 3⅜

**Above:** A 'gingerbread' house in Suffolk built in 1860.

**Right:** Ecclesiastical influences were strongly felt on many Gothic Revival houses.

**Top and above left:** Fretwork gables and contrasting-coloured brick quoins and lintels provide attractive decorative features.

**Above:** A cornice of different-coloured tiles adds decoration to an ordinary roof, as do the patterned ridge tiles.

A variety of wall tiles illustrating some of the floral motifs popular in the Victorian era.

From the 1860s, terracotta became a popular material for decorative features. On Queen Anne-style houses, sculptured terracotta panels with geometric or floral motifs were inset into external walls, under the eaves, or between doors and windows. Terracotta was also used to face ballustrades.

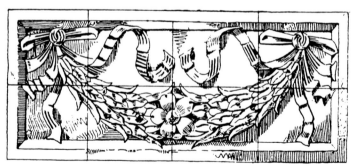

Decorative terracotta finials were popular features on roofs and porches.

**Above:** In the second half of the nineteenth century encaustic-tiled pavements in lozenge patterns and geometric shapes appeared on the front paths of many suburban houses. As well as being durable, their warm, natural clay colours were also welcoming.

**Opposite top left**: Late Victorian porch entrances were often inset with decorative tiled wall panels.

**Opposite top right:** An example of how different patterned brickwork was used by Victorian architects to enliven the exterior of a house.

**Opposite below:** Panels of patterned tiles were also to be found on external walls.

Porches, which provided an impressive-looking entrance as well as giving shelter from the weather, were a popular features of Victorian houses. A variety of designs were in evidence throughout the nineteenth century.

These pages show details of two designs for an American porch, c. 1880, with a variety of possible supporting columns.

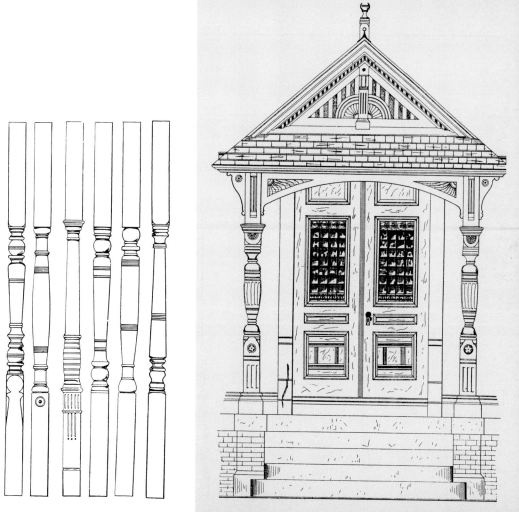

English porches ranged from stately structures with
classical forms to simple bracketed canopies.

**Opposite:** A Victorian Gothic porch.

**Centre above:** In the first half of the nineteenth century, it was fashionable to view what was happening outside from graceful ironwork balconies such as this.

**Above and centre bottom:** With improvements in mass production, intricately worked cast-iron porches, balconies and railings became widely available during the Victorian era.

Victorian designs for ornamental
verandahs and balconies.

Railings and gates became more decorative from the 1820s with the increase in the variety of ironwork being mass produced. The publication of pattern books by Coalbrookdale, Carron and other firms meant that the Victorian house-owner was greeted with a wealth of items from which to choose.

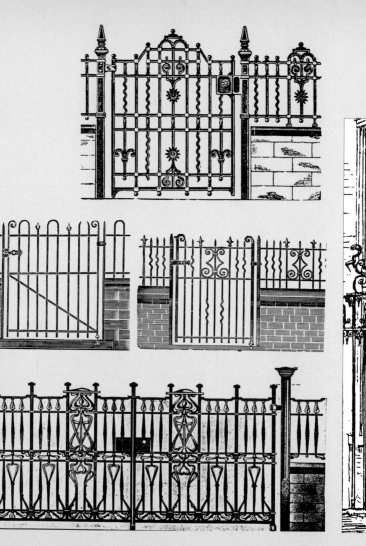

Ornamental cast-iron gates and railings announced to the outside world the status of the family within; thus the more elaborately decorated they were, the better. The sinuous forms of some Art Nouveau designs were particularly suited to wrought ironwork – for example, the bottom gates on the opposite page.

To delineate the boundaries of their property, Victorians could choose from a wide variety of railings, from simple sticks with a decorative top to more ornate patterns.

**Above:** The style of this graceful Georgian fanlight, with its Coade stone voussoirs, was copied on early Victorian buildings. Later, stucco was used instead of stone.

**Right and opposite:** Whatever the style or status of the house, an imposing front door inset with glass panels was an essential feature of most Victorian entrances.

Cast iron was the popular material for door
furniture in the first half of the nineteenth century.

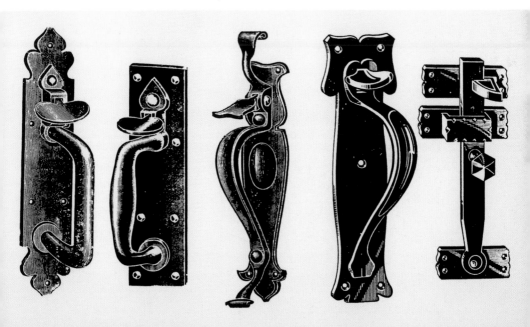

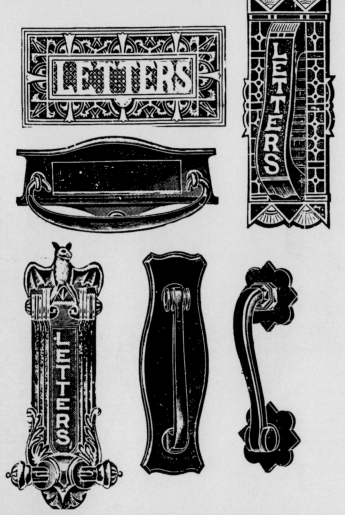

By the 1850s the use of brass door furniture had become more widespread, and shining letterboxes added the finishing touches to many front doors.

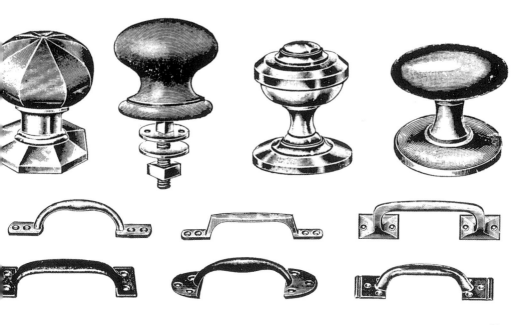

**Left:** An ornate early Victorian door knocker, with a ram's head, embellishes a solid wood-panelled door.

**Above:** Gleaming brass door furniture found its way on to many front doors from the 1850s, especially now that even the middle classes had servants to polish it.

**Left:** This front entrance, set into the bay of the house, combines many of the popular design features of the late-Victorian period.

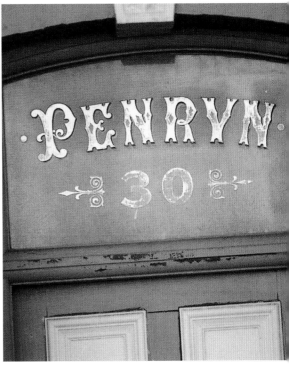

**Opposite:** Stained-glass panels became very fashionable in the 1880s, inspired by William Morris's designs for this revived craft. *London Door Company.*

**Right:** An Italianate front door, c.1860, is framed by classical marble columns.

**Above:** The name and number of this house etched into the fanlight decorate an ordinary front door.

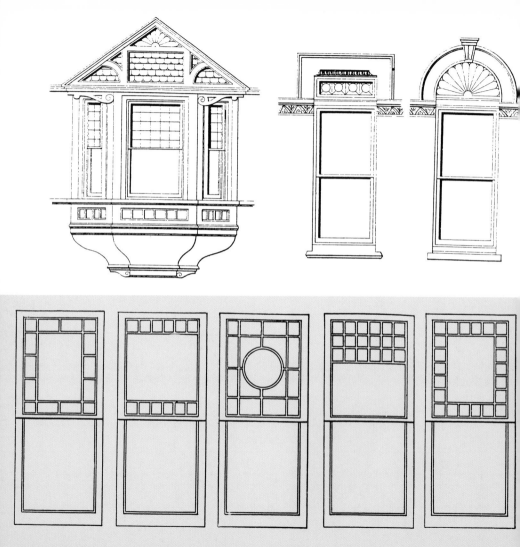

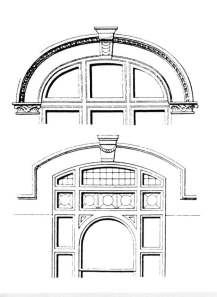

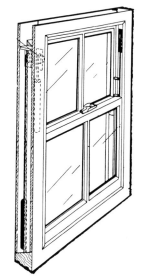

In the 1870s vernacular architects began reviving the fashion for oriel windows (opposite top left) and small leaded panes of glass, often with stained glass inset into their upper panels. Window surrounds and arch-heads were also highly decorated to complement the style of building.

**Left:** A four-paned vertical-sliding sash window, the most common form of window in the mid-Victorian era.

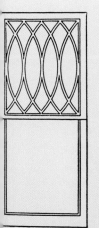
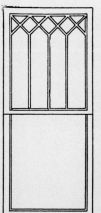
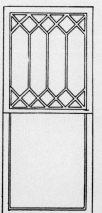
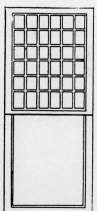
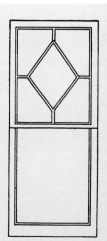

A late-Victorian terraced house with a square bay and Queen Anne-style sash windows.

Lancet-shaped glass panes were often inset into a square-framed sash window to provide a Gothic feature in the mid- to late-nineteenth century.

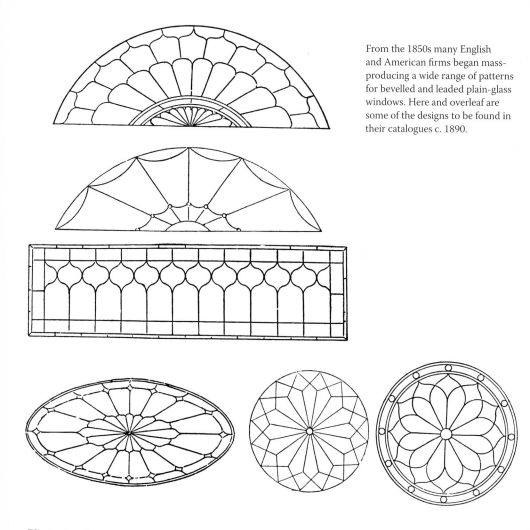

From the 1850s many English and American firms began mass-producing a wide range of patterns for bevelled and leaded plain-glass windows. Here and overleaf are some of the designs to be found in their catalogues c. 1890.

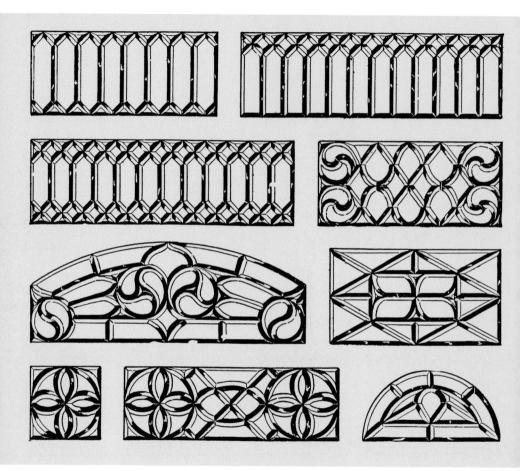

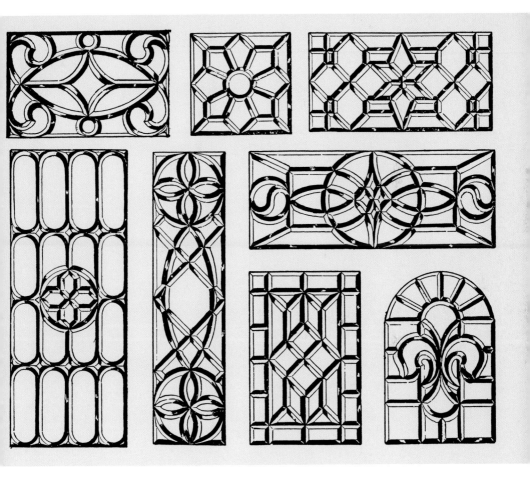

**Above:** A round-arched Italianate-style window with a decorative ironwork window guard.

**Left top:** The warm brown colours and floral theme are typical of the stained-glass windows designed by the Arts and Crafts movement from the 1870s.

**Left bottom:** Some late Victorian homes adopted the use of external shutters.

**Above:** Simple lancet windows, Gothic arched window hoods and wooden decoration give this house a medieval look.

**Above right:** Many Victorian houses had square sash windows on one storey with rounded Italianate ones on another.

Stained-glass window and door panels enjoyed great popularity in the nineteenth century. However, as mass-produced copies replaced individually hand-crafted windows and the market became flooded, a backlash ensued: by the start of the Edwardian era, 'pure' glass, not decorated, was the vogue.

A variety of patterns for both plain and stained-glass windows, manufactured by Victorian firms in the late nineteenth century.

# Chapter 2

# Hallways, Stairs, Landings and Bedrooms

*'The Entrance-Hall is an apartment of so many characteristic varieties that it may almost be taken as a criterion of the class to which the house belongs. In a case of the least ambitious order it will be no more than a wide passage from the Entrance-Hall to the staircase ... whereas in a first-class Mansion it will be a spacious and perhaps stately apartment ... decorated with paintings and statuary, ancestral armour and the trophies of the chase.'*

Robert Kerr, *The Gentleman's House* (1864)

**Previous page:** The hall at 18 Stafford Terrace, the home of *Punch* cartoonist Linley Sambourne. The carpet was designed by John Henry Dearle for Morris & Co. c.1890.

The staircase at The Red House.

Victorian hallways were usually rather dim, with only a small amount of natural light coming through the fanlight or the door's stained-glass panels. This was supplemented by hanging oil or gas lanterns and wall brackets. The entrance hall was invariably decorated in strong, dark colours and potted plants in *jardinieres* were placed everywhere.

**Above:** Delicate hall chairs and benches were in fashion in the early Victorian period, but gave way to over-ornate furniture from the 1850s.

**Right:** One of William Morris's stained-glass panels.

**Far right:** 'Mural Decoration for a Dado', Charles Eastlake's design for a hall, 1878.

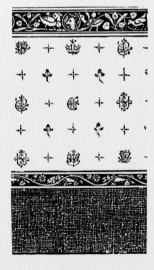

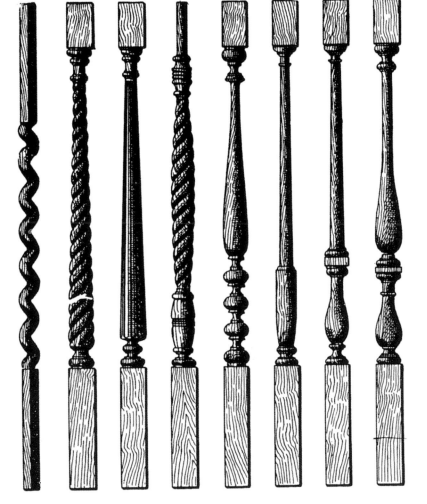

A selection
of designs for
wooden stair
balusters.

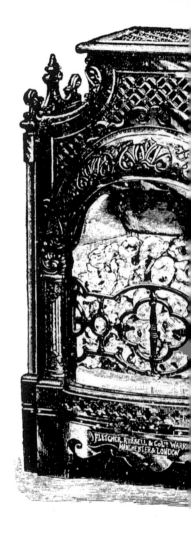

**Opposite:** This ornate cast-iron umbrella stand is typical of the style of hall furniture appearing from the 1850s.

**Centre and below:** Open fires and, later, radiators were a feature of many entrance halls, even narrow ones, as they provided warmth on entering the house.

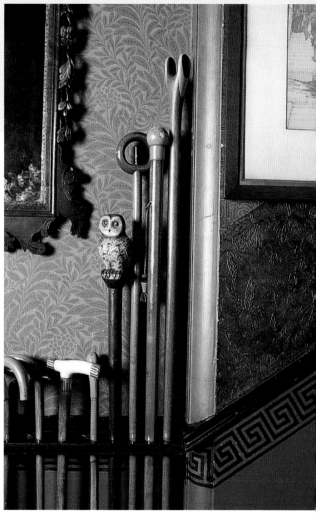

**Opposite:** An authentic-looking late Victorian hallway, with its geometrically patterned encaustic tiles, stained-glass front door and mahogany hall stand.

**Above:** Vestibules were not only another form of decoration but also provided practical insulation. Plain-glass panes were often inset into the vestibule door so that the rich colours and patterns of the stained-glass front door could be seen in the hallway.

**Right:** Dados with panels or decorated in a contrasting colour to the rest of the wall were a traditional feature of most Victorian hallways and landings from the 1870s. This one has been decorated in the popular colours of the time: sage green and burgundy.

In 1878 Charles Eastlake wrote: 'There can be little doubt that the best mode of treating a hall-floor ... is to pave it with encaustic tiles.' These are some of the geometric patterns and classically inspired mosiacs that were commercially available.

**Right**: Australia's ornamental cast-ironwork became world-famous from the 1880s. At Medley Hall near Melbourne, this intricately worked staircase leads down to a stunning encaustic-tiled hall floor.

**Below:** These encaustic-tiled pavements and borders produced by Maw & Co. of Salop were considered by Eastlake to be 'unrivalled'.

Even ordinary staircases were decorated with carved balusters and newel posts.

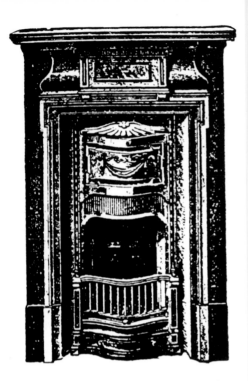

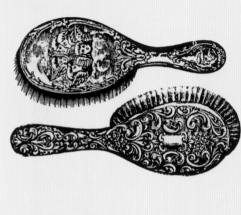

**Above:** Fireplaces became smaller and less ornate in the upper storeys of the house. The were normally made of wood or cast iron with a simple register grate and surround.

**Centre:** Hairbrushes and lamps that would have been found in a Victorian bedroom.

**Opposite:** Eastlake's 1878 design for an iron bedstead with a half-tester canopy.

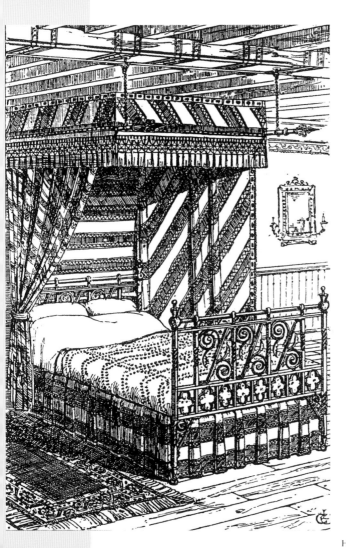

**Above:** Decorative light fittings.

**Right:** As concern grew that the heavy drapes of four-poster beds harboured dust and germs, half-testers with decorative canopies became fashionable.

**Centre:** Victorian wardrobes could be over two metres tall. By the 1890s, however, built-in furniture became popular.

**Below:** Dressing-tables were another main feature of the room and were usually placed in the bay of the window.

**Above:** There would often be several small tables covered with hand-made tablecloths, candles, mirrors, flowers and other objets in a Victorian bedroom.

**Above right:** Victorian bedrooms were feminine in character and filled with hand-made decorative objects, like this lace bedspread and scattered cushions. The stained-glass windows also give the room a period feel, although a Victorian bathroom would not have been en-suite with the bedroom.

**Opposite:** By the 1860s, simple brass beds such as this had become fashionable as they were considered to be more hygienic than draped half-testers.

Washstands, shaving stands, towel rails and dressing-tables were essential items of bedroom furniture. However, whilst the mid-Victorians indulged their love of over-decoration and fussy fabric treatments, even on dressing-tables, the Arts and Crafts movement preferred their furniture to be ornamental with simple carving, patterned tiles and detailed metalwork.

One can achieve a Victorian-style bedroom by finding original decorative items and pieces of furniture in antique and junk shops. Many traditional designs for lights, brass beds and fabrics are also being widely reproduced today. *Adrian Sankey*

A heavy, carved mahogany bed was the
most important item of furniture in a
mid-Victorian bedroom.

A selection of decorated washstands, which featured in the 1888 J.L. Mott Ironworks catalogue.

Wooden washstands, normally of mahogany, were permanently in the bedroom. Water jugs, soap dishes and wash bowls (opposite), decorated with flowers or Oriental designs were not only practical items but provided colour in the room.

# Chapter 3

# Living Rooms

*'In [the drawing room] ladies receive calls throughout the afternoon, and the family and their guests assemble before dinner. After dinner the ladies withdraw to it ... It is also the reception room for evening parties ... The character to be always aimed at in a drawing room is especial cheerfulness, refinement of elegance, and what is called lightness as opposed to massiveness. Decoration and furniture ought therefore to be comparatively delicate; in short, the rule in everything is this ... to be entirely ladylike.'*

Robert Kerr, *The Gentleman's House* (1864)

**Previous page:** An Aesthetic drawing room, c 1880, with its tripartite wall – dado, central filling and deep frieze, each of which would have been decorated in a different way and its plate rails displaying Oriental china.

**Opposite:** A handsome chimney-piece, like this Belgian rouge marble fireplace, c.1880, was felt to be essential in a Victorian dining room. This one at Wardlaw, near Melbourne, is complemented by a magnificent cornice and ceiling frieze.

**Centre:** An unusual feature of this white marble and enamel chimney piece is this elaborate circular over-mantel mirror.

**Left:** Seamless Axminster carpets were commercially manufactured to imitate Oriental rugs.

**Opposite and centre top:** The lines adopted by the Arts and Crafts movement reintroduced simplicity into the home, with a prefernce for plainer decoration and furniture made by old-fashioned joinery techniques.

**Centre bottom and below:** The High Victorians preferred fussy fringes and frills. Chairs were upholstered in floral patterns with lavish trimmings. Drawing-rooms were also filled with ornaments, plant stands and lamps.

**Above:** The light, feminine styles of the late-Regency period were still in evidence in early Victorian drawing-rooms.

**Opposite:** A Gothic Revival living room with original Victorian Gothic furniture.

In contrast to the High Victorian drawing-room with its lavish drapery and profusion of ornaments and furniture, Eastlake's favoured style was lighter and more 'aesthetic'. Many of the designs shown here and on pages 118–119 were recommended in his *Hints on Household Taste* of 1878.

A selection of drawing-room furniture, c. 1875.

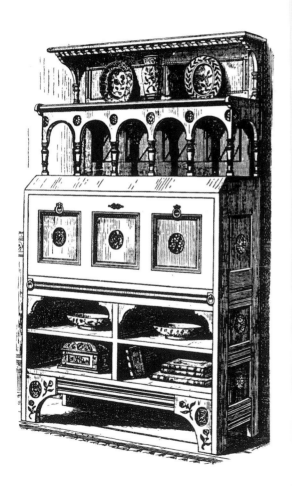

**Opposite:** In this Victorian reception room, decorated in floral patterns and sombre colours, every surface is adorned with bric-a-brac.

**Above:** A typical dining room with table laid for supper.

**Right top:**
A sideboard with
Gothic features.

**Right bottom:**
Examples of a
Gothic oak, a
mahogany and a
padded-damask
dining-room chairs.

**Opposite:**
A sideboard
designed by
Eastlake in 1878

Early Victorian dining-room tables were more elegant than the heavy mahogany ones favoured in the 1850s. However, from the late 1870s Eastlake and Arts and Crafts members began to look to Jacobean and other Old English designs for their tables.

**Left:** Victorian billiard rooms were masculine retreats and were usually decorated with wooden floors, real or simulated wood-panelled walls and dominant fireplaces.

**Above:** This 1880s fireplace and mantelpiece are made entirely of cast iron.

Eastlake's design for a
library bookcase, c. 1878

A Victorian billiard-room light to hang over the table. This design is till being manufactured today.

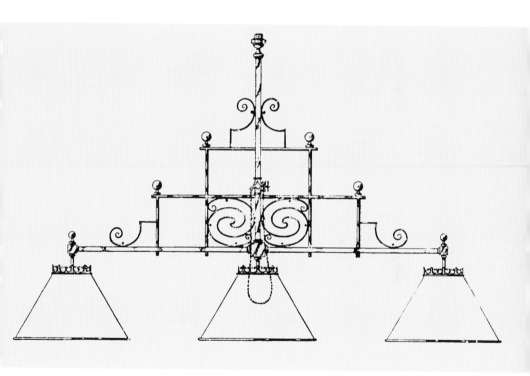

**Left:** Many libraries doubled up as studios where members of the household tried their hand at painting or sat for portraits. Sometimes paintings were displayed on an easel instead of hung on the wall.

**Above:** A late-Victorian bookstand.

**Opposite:** An 1880 design for the arrangement and decoration of a library.

# Chapter 4

# Kitchens and Bathrooms

*'It must be remembered that [the kitchen] is the great laboratory of every household, and that much of the "weal and woe" as far as regards bodily health depends upon the nature of the preparations concocted within its walls.'*

Mrs Beeton

**Below and opposite bottom:** Late
Victorian closed stoves.

**Opposite top:** This scullery sink would
have had a single cold tap and a wooden
draining board.

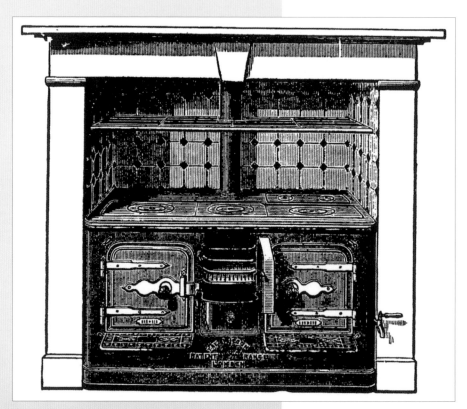

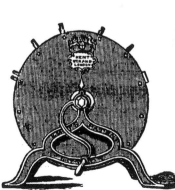

Jelly moulds, mangles and
knife sharpeners were
essential kitchen utensils.

**Left:** A traditional white porcelain butler's sink with a plate rack overhead. *Robinson & Cornish*

**Above:** The original fireplace and cooking range in the kitchen of Como House in Melbourne, Australia, c.1860.

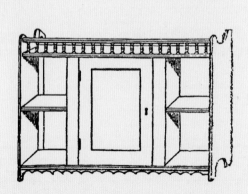
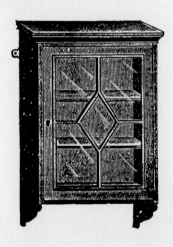

A range of small kitchen shelves, stoves and utensils that appeared in late-Victorian catalogues.

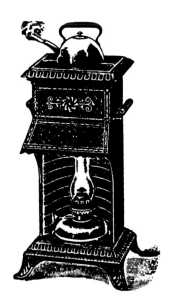

Cast-iron ranges with open fires and a closed oven for baking were gradually replaced by the 1840s with the more efficient closed stove. Mrs Beeton illustrated the American stove bottom right, in her *Book of Household Management*.

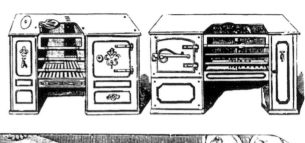

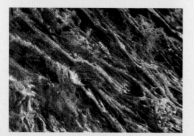

**Left:** Examples of *faux*-marbling widely used in Victorian times.

**Centre right:** By the end of the nineteenth century, kitchens and sculleries were tiled as concern for hygiene grew. The sink was usually sited under a window.

**Opposite top:** A modern kitchen can be given a period feel just by adding a cooking range. New Agas are available as are many original fittings that can be reconditioned. *Robinson & Cornish. Holden Heat plc.*

**Opposite bottom:** The kitchen range at Standen, in West Sussex, designed by Philip Webb in 1894. *National Trust*

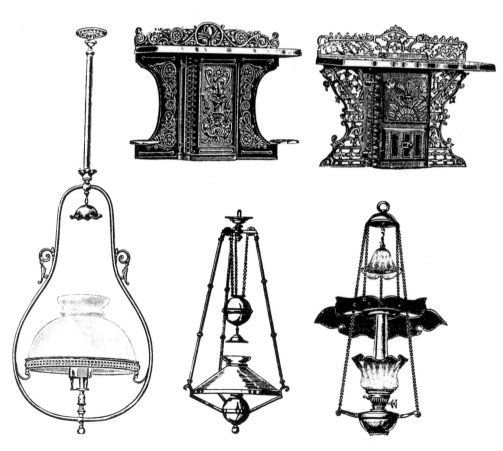

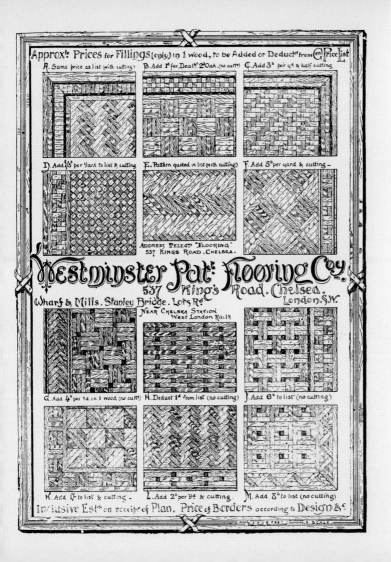

Approx: Prices for Fillings (only) in 1 wood, to be Added or Deducted from Gen.l Price List

A. Same price as list (with cutting)   B. Add 1ᵈ for Deal & 2ᵈ Oak (no cutt.)   C. Add 3ᵈ per y.ᵈ & half cutting

D. Add 1/8 per Yard to list & cutting   E. Pattern quoted in list (with cutting)   F. Add 5ᵈ per yard & cutting –

Address Teleg.ⁱ "Flooring"
537 Kings Road, Chelsea.

## Westminster Pat: Flooring Coy.
### 537 King's Road, Chelsea, London, S.W.

Wharf & Mills, Stanley Bridge, Lots Rᵈ
Near Chelsea Station
West London Railʸ

G. Add 4ᵈ per y.ᵈ in 1 wood (no cutt.)   H. Deduct 1ᵈ from list (no cutting)   J. Add 6ᵈ to list (no cutting)

K. Add 1½ᵈ to list & cutting –   L. Add 2ᵈ per y.ᵈ & cutting.   M. Add 8ᵈ to list (no cutting)

Inclusive Est.ⁿ on receipt of Plan. Price of Borders according to Design &c

**Opposite top:**
Elaborate decoration found its way into the kitchen with ornate cast-iron stove backs.

**Opposite bottom:**
Hanging oil or gas lamps were placed in the centre of the room over the kitchen table.

**Left:** Linoleum was the most popular type of flooring in the late-Victorian kitchen because it was durable and easy to keep clean. It was manufactured in a number of patterns, including imitation woods.

Recreating a Victorian bathroom, but with modern reproduction fittings. Gleaming brass, wood and antique accessories complete the overall scene.

In 1888 J.L. Mott Ironworks illustrated these baths in their catalogue. Their 'Eastlake' interior was decorated with carved mahogany cabinet work and hand-painted tiles.

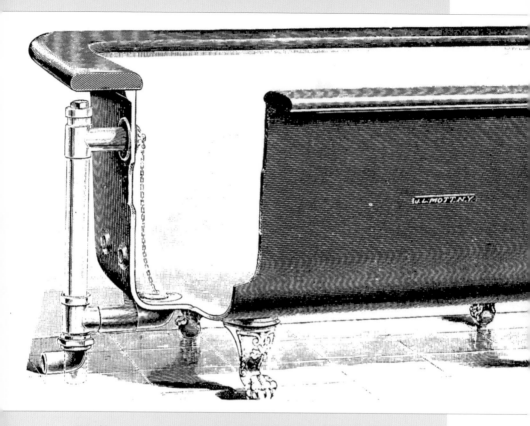

Portable cast-iron baths were replaced by fixed baths after 1870. Cast-iron baths, coated inside with white porcelain enamel, were initially encased in wood-panelled surrounds, but as hygiene became increasingly important in the 1880s, tubs began to be free-standing, with claw or ball feet, so that they could be washed underneath.

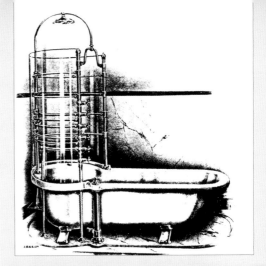

From the 1880s needle and spray showers became commercially available.

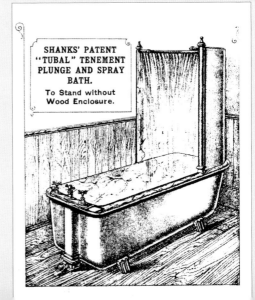

SHANKS' PATENT
"TUBAL" TENEMENT
PLUNGE AND SPRAY
BATH.

To Stand without
Wood Enclosure.

Before the 1880s, washstands were hidden in marble-topped mahogany cabinets. However, with increased interest in hygiene, fittings began to be exposed so that they could be cleaned easily. Original washstands can still be found in antique shops and then plumbed with modern fixtures.

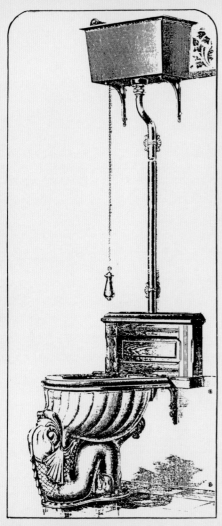

**Opposite:** 'The Dolphin' water closet, 1888.

**Centre and below:** By the end of the nineteenth century bathroom walls were tiled, with co-ordinating patterned borders, cornices and dado rails. Floors were also tiled and pipes were exposed. Interiors were plainer, but toilet bowls and bases were still targets for decoration.

**Left:** Stained-glass windows, original overmantel and wooden details can give a small bathroom or cloakroom a Victorian 'feel'.

**Opposite:** A pretty evocation of a Victorian-style bathroom. *BC Sanitan Pipe Dreams*

A selection of the bathroom accessories available from late-Victorian catalogues.

# Chapter 5
# Interior Details

*... 'a Gentleman's House ought to be not merely substantial, comfortable, convenient and well furnished, but fairly adorned'.*

Robert Kerr, *The Gentleman's House* (1864)

Dados were particularly used in hallways or dining rooms to protect the plastering, and would be treated in a number of ways. Larger houses used an embossed paper with a surface resembling leather, which came in a number of patterns, including the newly fashionable Japanese designs (centre and opposite). The centre of the wall was then decorated, usually with densely patterned wallpapers (above).

A false dado could be created in a high-ceilinged room by applying a chair rail to the walls and painting in the area between the rail and the skirting board. Picture rails were also added about three-quarters of the way to the ceiling in order to break up a large expanse of wall. the cornice or frieze then completed the wall, joining it with the ceiling.

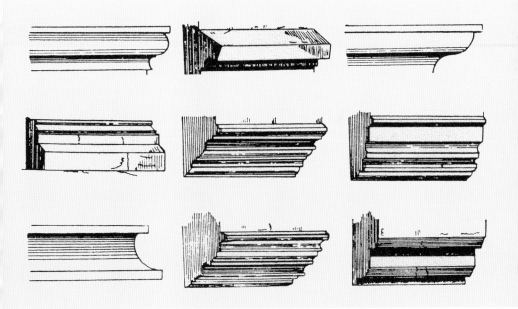

**Left:** Wall panelling was often inset with patterned wallpaper or trompe l'oeil decoration.

**Above:** Towards the end of the Victorian era, it was no longer fashionable for walls to be divided into three sections. One alternative style was floor-to-ceiling wall panels, decorated with heavily patterned wallpaper and edged with a narrow skirting board and cornice.

Once fibrous plaster became commercially available, decorative cornices and friezes began to appear on the walls and ceilings of most Victorian rooms. Designs ranged from classical motifs to intricately moulded floral patterns.

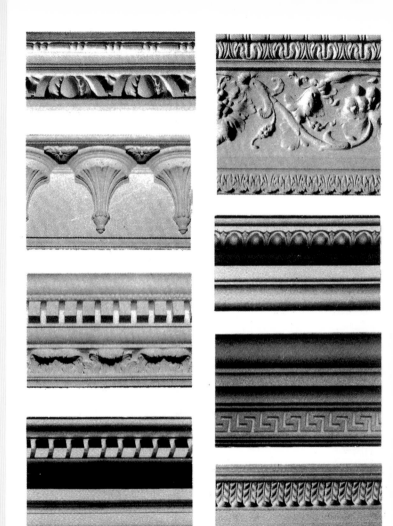

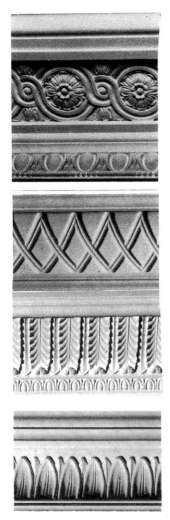

Decorative brackets and ceiling medallions, echoing the design of the cornice, were also popular adornments.

**Opposite:** To recreate the feel of an authentic Victorian home it is important to remember their love of elaborate decoration which they applied to every available surface.

**Left top:** This dado and Victorian cast-iron radiator are painted in a traditional burgundy colour. The dado border is a Greek key pattern.

**Left bottom:** The Victorians' love of decoration extended to their ceilings with the use of heavily carved and gilded friezes.

A simple panelled door would be embellished with brass door furniture, decorated panels and elaborate door frames.

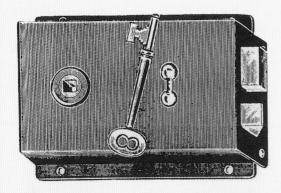

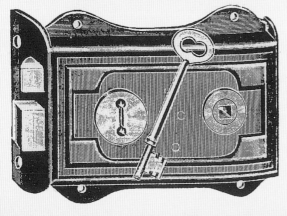

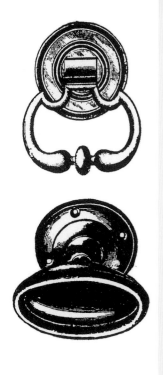

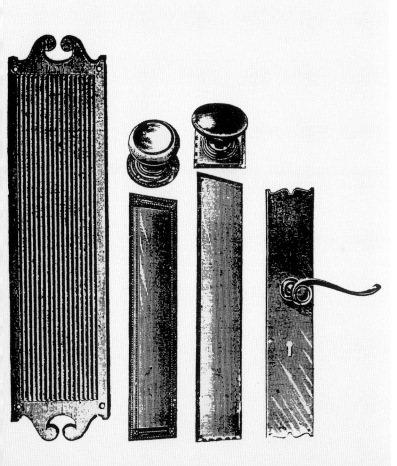

Door furniture was usually of gleaming brass, with elegant handles, elaborate escutcheons and finger plates in the varying styles of the period. Painted porcelain or plain china finger plates and door knobs were also popular.

Two very extreme door treatments, with grained and stencilled panels, ornate brass door furniture and heavily draped *portières*.

The Arts and Crafts and the Aesthetic movements decorated their walls with deep-patterned friezes and borders.

**Above left:** William Morris's 'Wallflower' design, a pattern of decorative, curvaceous forms, was first produced in 1890.

**Above right:** His 'Willow Bough' wallpaper design, first produced in the 1890s.

An early advertisement for Lincrusta, which was first available in 1877.

# LINCRUSTA-WALTON

### The *Original* "Sunbury" make.

*"Jacobean" Dining Hall—illustrating the use of Lincrusta Oak Panelling, Lignomur Rough-cast Frieze and Anaglypta High Relief Ceiling and Cornice.*

*Specialities—*

## Wainscot Panelling.  Glazed Tile Decorations.

Practically indestructible for Walls and Ceilings and is largely used as a substitute for Wood and Tiles.  Will not crack or warp.

# LIGNOMUR & CAMEOID

Embossed Decorations with a clean White finish.  A large and varied assortment of designs for Dadoes, Fillings, Friezes, Ceilings and Cornices in rolls of 24 yards.

**The Wall Paper Manufacturers, Ltd.**
(Lincrusta-Walton Branch),

Darwen,

Lancs.

**The Wall Paper Manufacturers, Ltd.**
(Lignomur Branch),

Old Ford, Bow,

London, E.3.

*Showrooms for all Relief Materials at 1 Newman St., London, W.1.*

Wooden Venetian blinds and shutters were often to be found on Victorian windows. In the High Victorian era, they were then covered with several layers of curtaining.

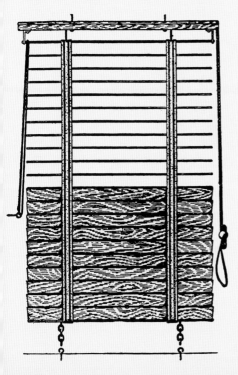

By the late 1870s Eastlake was decrying the fashion for 'heavy and artificial folds', and advocating simple arrangements for curtains and *portieres*.

Elaborate drapes and ruched pelmets evoke the atmosphere of a
Victorian drawing room. *Lighting Designs Ltd. Osborne & Little plc*

Parquet floors – waxed strips of contrasting-coloured hardwoods with different patterned borders – were available in a wide variety of designs from the 1870s. Oriental rugs would be scattered on top.

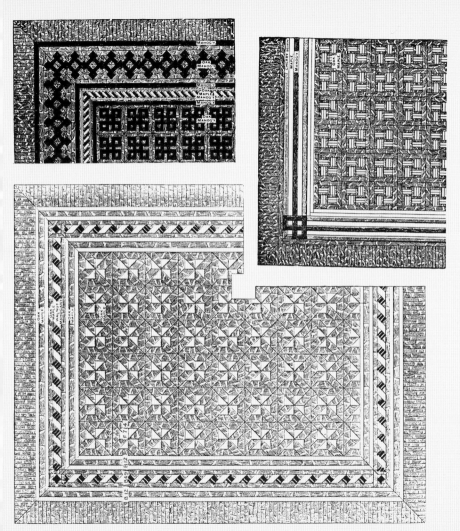

The floors of the main
reception rooms in a
Victorian house were laid
with deeply patterned
carpets or large rugs in
strong, warm colours. The
fashion prevailed for most
of the Victorian era.

Each room in a Victorian house had a fireplace in it, which not only provided heat but also formed the focal point of the room. Therefore, as H.W. and A. Arrowsmith wrote in their *House Decorator's and Painter's Guide* in 1840, 'Too much labour cannot be bestowed on the decoration of the chimneypiece, as it is the part of the room to which the attention is chiefly drawn.'

A range of mid- to late-Victorian cast-iron register grates and chimneypieces. These grates were developed for burning the newly available cheap coal and had a metal plate across the chimney, which regulated the amount of smoke and created a smaller draught.

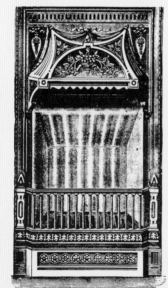

**Opposite:** Classically inspired chimneypieces, wooden overmantels and simple mantelpieces were covered with the statues, china and other ornaments so loved by the Victorians. Patterned tiles were then inset into the sides.

**Left:** In the 1880s cast-iron houses and stoves were exported to Australia during the Gold Rush. This surviving example has planks from the packing cases lining its walls.

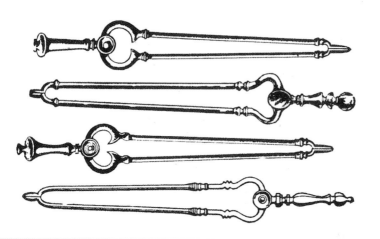

**Left and below:** Fire accessories were manufactured to complement the different styles of fireplaces they served.

Early Victorian fire surrounds were made predominantly of marble, carved stone or wood. As cast iron grates became more common, new semi-circular shapes (opposite) grew in popularity.

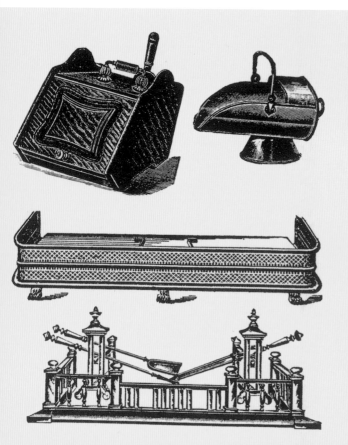

Ironwork, brass and copper fire accessories, including gleaming fenders, andirons, fire-backs, coal scuttles, fire-irons and fire-dogs manufactured in the different styles prevalent throughout the century sat beside the fireplace, adding to its overall decoration. Needlepoint firescreens embroidered by the women of the household completed the scene.

The fireplaces illustrated here and on page 206 were designed by
Philip Webb for Standen House, Sussex, in 1894. Now owned by the
National Trust, it is the only one of his houses to have survived and is
a fine example of the architecture and interior decoration adopted by
William Morris and his followers.

**Above:** in the 1860s and 1870s mantelpieces had been swathed in material to match the lavish furnishing in the rest of the room. However, draped mantelpieces fell out of fashion towards the end of the century.

Decorative cast-iron stoves were more common in Europe and America than in England. These styles appeared in a New York manufacturer's catalogue for 1898.

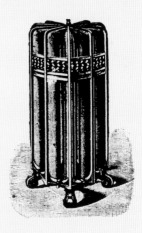

Central heating via cast-iron radiators was developed towards the end of the nineteenth century. However, because of their expense, radiators only appeared in wealthy homes.

Oil and gas hanging lights, wall brackets and table lamps provided the dim Victorian house with a modicum of light. When electricity introduced brighter light into the home In the 1880s, coloured glass,in the style of Louis Comfort Tiffany, and hand-painted porcelain shades became popular to soften the glare. These traditional Victorian designs are still being produced today.

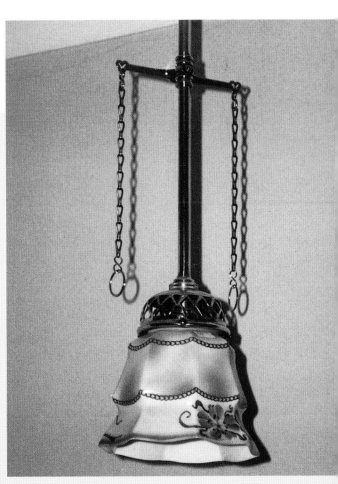

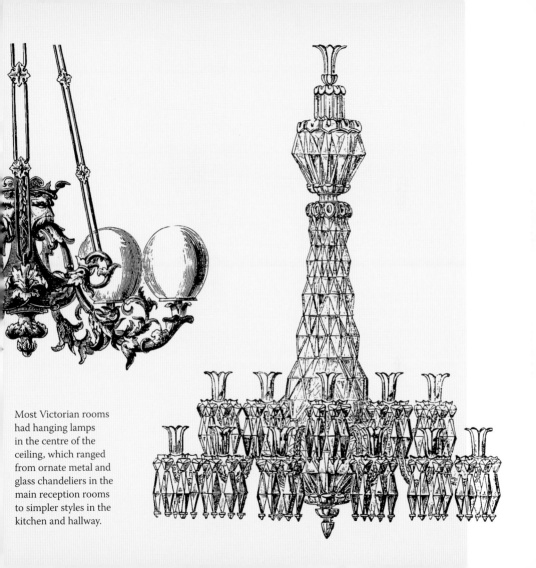

Most Victorian rooms had hanging lamps in the centre of the ceiling, which ranged from ornate metal and glass chandeliers in the main reception rooms to simpler styles in the kitchen and hallway.

Late Victorian light fittings were enhanced by intricately moulded brass and sinuously curved and sculptured Art Nouveau metalwork.

Over-dressed fabric lampshades and patterned beading and fringes were a traditional feature of High Victorian style. It was not until later in the century that more delicate glass shades began to appear. However, some oil lamps on bases shaped like classical urns and columns had plainer glass bowls.

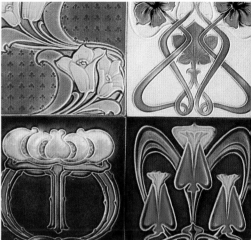

Flowers, foliage and birds were popular subjects on Victorian decorative tiles.

**Opposite left:** *Original Style* Victorian picture tiles.

**Above and left:** *Original Style* 'Birds and Butterfly'. Art Nouveau motifs (above) and William Morris floral patterns (top left and left) looked particularly effective on ceramic tilework.

In 1840 Herbert Minton developed a method for making encaustic tiles – inlaying different coloured clays and fusing them together during firing – and soon these tiles were being commercially manufactured. Fleur-de-lys and trefoil patterns, as well as many geometric mosaics, were produced in the natural colours of the clay – white, black, red and cream being the normal hues – with blue, green and lilac becoming available later through the use of chemical dyes.

A range of elaborate encaustic tile patterns to be found in the halls of wealthier households.

# Chapter 6

# The Victorian Garden

*'Heated to a pleasant temperature, full of bright and rare blooms, the gentle breath of sweet-scented gardenias and tuberoses pervades the atmosphere. Cages of many-coloured foreign birds, a gleam of Moorish lamps against the greenery overhead, comfortable lounges, wickerwork tables Turkish rugs strewn on the tesselated floor – all combine to make a delightful place in which to while away Time with books or work.'*

Mrs Alexander Fraser, novelist and hostess,
describing her Sussex conservatory, c. 1880

The formal Italian garden, which was popular throughout the first half of Victoria's reign, was replaced in the 1870s by the desire to return to a more natural look. However, in the 1890s garden designers reintroduced a degree of formality by the use of such features as trellised walkways (opposite).

**Previous page:** The conservatory was an ideal Victorian innovation, which combined new technological developments in ironwork and glazing with the nineteenth century love of scientific and botanical exploration. *Town & Country Conservatories*

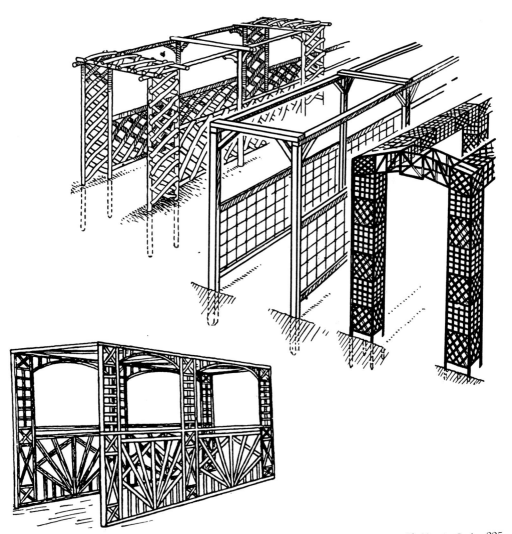

FLOWERING SHRUBS

SEAT      TREE

BIRD
COTE

RHODODENDRONS

TREE            LILIUMS

AZALEAS

SCREEN

ROSE BORDER

PERGOLA ARCHES

William Robinson, who started *The Garden* in 1871, was the most importan garden writer of the time. Herbaceous borders and informal beds full of wild flowers were features of his gardens, as were rustic paths of gravel, stone or grass.

The Victorians placed their conservatories so that their exotic plants and classical decor could be admired by guests in the main drawing room. As well as being filled with plants, the grand conservatories also contained cast-iron or wicker settees, chairs and tables, fountains, statues and urns. Further decoration was added with patterned floor tiles, ornate iron details and stained- or etched-glass panes.

An authentic conservatory can be restored or added on to any Victorian home today because many of the original designs are being reproduced once more. *Town & Country Conservatories*

# Stockists

## Information & Advice

Architectural Salvage
Netley House
Gomshall Surrey GU5 2QA
Tel: 01483 203221
Fax: 01483 202911
Email: admin@handr.co.uk
Website: www.handr.co.uk/
salvage_home.html
Index of architectural items. For a
fee of £10 they will put buyers in
touch with sellers. They do not keep
items for sale.

British Decorators Association
32 Coton Road
Nuneaton
Warwickshire CV11 5TW
Tel: 01203 353776
Over 1,000 members who specialize
in the decoration of period homes.

The Brooking Collection School
of Architecture/Construction
University of Greenwich
Avery Hill Campus
Mansion Site  Bexley Road
London SE9 2PQ
Tel: 020 8331 9312
Fax: 020 8331 9105
Email: j.lynch@gre.ac.uk

Website: www.dartfordarchive.
org.uk/technology/art_
brooking.shtml
Unique record of the development
of period detail. Information and
advice available.

Redundant Church Furnishings
Church Commissioners
1 Millbank London SW1 P 3JZ
Tel: 020 7898 1619/20/23
Email: commissioners.enquiry@
c-of-e.org.uk.

Will supply contents register listing
items from redundant churches.

The Victorian Society
1 Priory Gardens
Bedford Park
London W4 1TT
Tel: 020 8747 5890
Email: admin@victoriansociety.
org.uk
Advice on restoration and
preservation of Victorian buildings.

## Architectural Antiques & Salvage

Ace Demolition & Salvage
Barrack Road
West Parley
Nr Hurn
Wimborne
Dorset BH22 8UB
Tel: 01202 579222

Fax: 01202 58204
Email: equiries@acedemo.co.uk
Website: www.acedemo.co.uk

Alexander the Grate
126–128 Donegal Pass
Belfast B17 1BZ
Tel: 028 9023 2041
Website:
www.alexander-the-grate.com

Andy Thornton
Architectural Antiques
Ainleys Industrial Estate
Elland
West Yorks HXS 9JP
Tel: 01422 375595
Fax: 01422 377455
Email: email@andythornton.com
Website: www.andythornton.com

Baileys Architectural Antiques
The Engine Shed

Ashburton Industrial Estate
Ross-on-Wye
Herefordshire HR9 7BW
Tel: 01989 563015
Website:
www.baileyshomeandgarden.com

Barewood Trading Company
1–5 Laws Court
Belfast
County Antrim  BT1 1QS
Tel: 02890 245618

Bridgwater Reclamation Ltd.
Old Co-op Dairy
Monmouth Street
Bridgwater
Somerset TA6 5EH
Tel: 01278 424636

Brighton Architectural Salvage
33/34 Gloucester Road
Brighton Sussex BN1 4AQ

Tel: 01273 681656

Bygones Architectural
Reclamation (Canterbury) Ltd.
Nackington Road
Canterbury
Kent CT47BA
Tel: 0800 0433012 /
+44 1 227 767 453
Fax: 01227 762153
Email: Bob@Bygones.net

Cantabrian Antiques
& Architectural Salvage
16 Park Street
Lynton
North Devon
Tel: 01598 753282

Churchill's Architectural
Salvage
212 Old Kent Road
London SE1 5TY

Conservation Building
Products Ltd.
Forge Works
Forge Lane
Cradley Heath
Warley
West Midlands B64 5AL
Tel: 01384 569551
Email: info@conservation
buildingproducts.co.uk
Website: www.conservation
buildingproducts.co.uk

T. Crowther & Son Ltd.
282 North End Road
Fulham
London SW6 1NH

Cumbria Architectural Salvage
Birks Hill
Raughton Head
Carlisle
Cumbria CA5 7DH
Tel: 01697 476420

Dorset Reclamation
Cow Drove
Bere Regis
Wareham
Dorset BH20 7JZ
Tel: 01929 472200
Fax: 01929 472292
Email: info@
dorsetreclamation.co.uk

Website:
www.dorsetreclamation.co.uk/

Edinburgh Architectural
Salvage Yard (EASY)
Unit 6 Couper Street
off Coburg Street
Leith
Edinburgh EH6 6HH
Tel: 0141 556 7772/
+44 131 554 7077
Fax: +44 44 131 554 3070
Website:
www.easy-arch-salv.co.uk

Fens Restoration
46 Lots Road
Chelsea
London SW10 0QF
Tel: 020 7352 9883

The Furniture Cave
533 King's Road
London SW10 OTZ
Website:
www.furniturecave.co.uk

The House Hospital
14a Winders Road
Battersea
London
SW11 3HE
Tel: 020 7223 3179
Website:

www.thehousehospital.com

Hallidays Antiques Ltd.
The Old College
Dorchester-on-Thames
Oxon OX10 7HL
Tel: 01865 340028/68
Fax: +44 (0)1865 341149
Email: antiques@hallidays.com
Website: www.hallidays.com

Havenplans Architectural
Emporium
The Old Station
Station Road
Killamarsh
Sheffield
South Yorks S31 8EN
Tel: 0114 248 9972

LASSco
St Michael's Church
Mark Street
Shoreditch
London EC2A 5ER
Tel: 020 7749 9944
Fax: 020 7749 9941
Email: st.michaels@lassco.co.uk
Website: www.lassco.co.uk

Malton Reclamation & Sales
46 Hatchpond Road
Nuffield Industrial Estate
Poole

Dorset DH17 7JZ
Tel: 01202 672248

Oxford Architectural Antiques
16–18 London Street
Faringdon
Oxon SN7 7AA
Tel: 01367 242268
Fax:+44 (0)1367 242268
Email: michael@
oxfordarchitectural.co.uk
Website:
www.oxfordarchitectural.co.uk

The Pumping Station
Penarth Road
Cardiff
South Glam CF1 7TT
Tel: 02920 221085
Email:
info@the-pumpingstation.co.uk

Reclaimed Materials
Northgate White Lund
Industrial Estate
Morecambe
Lancs LA3 3AY
Tel: 01524 69094

R & R Reclamation
Bluebell Farm
Laughton Road
Blyton
Gainsborough

Lincs DN21 3LQ
Tel: 01427 628 753/07798 837 711
Email: rnrreclaim@fsmail.net
Website:
www.rr-reclamation.co.uk

Romsey Reclamation
Station Approach
Railway Station
Romsey
Hants S051 8DU
Tel: 01794 524174

Seymours Architectural Salvage
17 Beck Street
Portsea
Portsmouth
Hants PO1 3AN
Tel: 023 9286 4889

Solopark Ltd.
The Old Railway Station
Station Road
Nr Pampisford
Cambs CB2 4HB
Tel: 01223 834663

Walcot Reclamation
108 Walcot Street
Bath
Avon BA1 5BG
Tel: 01225 444404
Fax: 01225 448163

Email: rick@walcot.com
Website: www.walcot.com

Wells Reclamation Company
The Old Cider Farm
Wells Road
Coxley
Nr Wells
Somerset BA5 1 RQ
Tel: 01749 677087
Fax: 01749 671089
Email:
enquiries@wellsreclamation.com
Website:
www.wellsreclamation.co.uk

Wilson Reclamation Services
Yewtree Barn
Newton-in-Lartmel
nr Grange-over-Sands
Cumbria CA11 6JU
Tel: 01539 531498
Fax: 01539 539870
Email: wrs@yewtreebarn.co.uk
Website:
www.yewtreebarn.co.uk

## Mouldings

A B C Studios
(Plaster Mouldings) Ltd.
Oxford Mews
Oxford Lane
Cardiff

South Glamorgan CF24 3DU
Tel: 029 20482886
Fax: 029 20482886

Allied Guilds
Unit 19 Reddicap
Trading Estate
Coleshill Road
Sutton Coalfield
West Midlands B75 7BU
Tel: 0121 329 2874
Fax: 0121 311 1883

Architectural and Industrial GRP
29 High Street
Hampton Wick
Kingston upon Thames
Surrey KT1 4DA
Tel: 020 8977 8203
Fax: 01932 830274
Website: www.trylining.com

Architectural Mouldings Ltd.
Southbrook Place
Southbrook Road
Gloucester GL4 3YY
Tel: 01452 300071

Aristocast Originals Ltd.
2 Wardsend Road
Sheffield
South Yorkshire S6 1RQ
Tel: 0114 232 7018
Fax: 0114 234 4885

Artistic Plastercraft
Lyndhurst Studios
16–18 Lyndhurst Road
Bath
Avon BA2 3JH
Tel: 01225 315404
Email: lawr@supanet.com
Website:
www.artisticplastercraft.com

H & F Badcock
(Fibrous & Solid Plastering) Ltd.
Unit 9
57 Sandgate Road
Old Kent Road
Peckham
London SE15 1LE
Tel: 020 7639 0304
Fax: 020 7358 1239

Bangor Plaster Mouldings
21 Drumhirk Avenue
Conlig
Newtownards BT23 7PZ
Tel: 028 91451331

Copley Decor Ltd. Unit
1 Leyburn Business Park
Leyburn
North Yorkshire DL8 5QA
Tel: 01969 623410
Fax: 01969 624398
Email:
mouldings@copleydecor.co.uk

Website: www.copleydecor.com

Craigavon Cornicing Site
11 Ulster Street Industrial Area
Ulster Street Lurgan BT67 9RN
Tel: 02838 342222

F H Crocker
Crozier Road
Mutley
Plymouth
Devon PL4 7LN
Tel: 01752 661851

W G Crotch
10 Tuddenham Avenue
Ipswich
Suffolk IP4 2HE
Tel: 01473 250349
Fax:  01473 213180

L Grandison & Son
Innerleithen Road
Peebles
Tweeddale EH45 8BA
Tel: 01721720212
Website: www.lgrandisonand-
son.com/contactus

BA Hallidays
The Old College
Dorchester-on-Thames
Oxon OX9 8HL
Tel: 01865 340028

Fax: 01865 341149

E J Harmer & Co. Ltd.
19A Birkbeck Hill
London SE21 8JS
Tel: 020 8670 1017
Fax: 020 8766 6026
Website: www.ejharmer.co.uk

Locker & Riley Ltd.
Capital House
Bruce Groce
Wickford
Essex SS11 8DB
Tel: 01268 574100
Fax: 01268 574101

London Fine Art Plaster
7–9 Audrey Street
London E2 8QH
Tel: 01708 252400
Fax: 01708 252401
Email: heritage@lfap.co.uk
Website: www.lfap.co.uk

Malvern Studios
56 Cowleigh Road
Malvern
Worcs WR14 1QD
Tel: 01684 574913
Fax: 01684 569475
Email:
malvern.studios@btinternet.com
Website: www.malvernstudios.co.uk

E G Millar (Plastering) Ltd.
54 Hawkwood Crescent
Chingford London E4 7PJ
Tel: 020 85290431

Nicholl Plaster Mouldings
81 Knockbracken Road
Castlereach BT6 9SP
Tel: 02890 448410

Regency Moulding
23A Brendon Road
Bridgwater TA6 3QW
Tel: 01278 456150

Riverside Mouldings
Unit 18 Riverside Industrial
Estate
Riverway
London SE10 OBH

George Rome
(Ornamental Plasterwork) Ltd.
Unit 27–29 Carnoustie Place
Glasgow G5 8PH
Tel: 0141 429 8460
Website:
www.georgeromeplasterers.
com
Email: sastirling@
georgeromeplasterers.com

Stevensons of Norwich Ltd.
Roundtree Way

Norwich
Norfolk NR7 8SH
Tel: 01603 400824
Fax: 01603 405113
Email: info@stevensons-of-
norwich.co.uk
Website:
www.stevensons-of-
norwich.co.uk

## Tiles

A G Ceramics
Arlington Business Park
Whittle Way
Stevenage SG1 2BD
Tel: 01438 315 400
Fax: 01438 740 338
Website:
www.agceramics.co.uk

Sally Anderson (Ceramics) Ltd.
Parndon Mill
Harlow
Essex CM20 2HP
Tel: 01279 420982
Fax:  01279 415075
Email:
info@sally-anderson.co.uk
Website:
www.sally-anderson.co.uk

Bernard J Arnull &
Company Limited

17–21 Sunbeam Road
Park Royal
London NW10 6JP
Tel: 0208 965 6094
Fax: 0208 961 1585
Email:
enquiries@bernardarnull.co.uk
Website:
www.bernardarnull.co.uk

The Art Tile Company Ltd.
Etruria Tile Works
Garner Street
Etruria
Stoke-on-Trent

Fired Earth
3 Twyford Mill
Oxford Road
Adderbury
Nr Banbury
Oxfordshire OX17 3SX
Tel: 01295 812088
Fax:  01295 810832
Email:
enquiries@firedearth.com
Website: www.firedearth.com

Flooring Supplies Ltd.
Bernard Works
Bernard Road
London N15 4NX
Tel: 020 8808 3011
Fax: 020 88011546

H & R Johnson Tiles Ltd.
Harewood Street
Tunstall Stoke-on-Trent
Staffordshire ST6 5JZ
Tel: 01782 575575
Fax: 01782 577377 FPS
Website:
http://www.johnson-tiles.com

Maw & Co Ltd.
Unit 5b
Sneyd Trading Estate
Stoke-On-Trent
Staffordshire ST6 2EB
Tel: 01782 577250
Website: www.mawandco.com

Original Style
Falcon Road
Sowton Industrial Estate
Exeter EX2 7IF
Tel: 01392 473000
Fax: 01392 473003
Website: www.originalstyle.com
Email: info@originalstyle.com

Paris Ceramics
583 Kings Road Chelsea
London SW6 2EH
Tel: 020 7371 7778
Fax: 020 7371 8395
Email: london@
parisceramics.com
Website: www.parisceramics.com

Dennis Ruabon Ltd.
Haford Tileries
Ruabon
Wrexham LL14 6ET
Tel: 01978 842283
Fax: 01978 843276
Email:
salesenq@dennisruabon.co.uk
Website:
www.dennisruabon.co.uk

## Fireplaces

Acquisitions Fireplaces Ltd.
24–26 Holmes Road London
NW5 3AB
Tel: 020 7482 2949
Fax: 020 7267 4361
Website:
www.acquisitions.co.uk

Aga Rayburn
PO Box 30 Ketley
Telford Shropshire
Tel: 01952 642000
Website:
www.aga-rayburn.co.uk

Amazing Grates
Phoenix House
61–63 High Road
East Finchley
London N2 8AB

Tel: 0208 883 9590/
0208 883 6017
Fax: 0208 365 2053
Website:
www.gatwoodandelcombe.com

Anglia Fireplaces
Anglia House
Kendal Court
Cambridge Road
Impington
Cambridge CB24 9YS
Tel: 01223 234713
Email: sales@fireplaces.co.uk
Website: www.fireplaces.co.uk

Cantabrian Antiques
16 Park Street
Lynton
Devon EX35 6BY
Tel: 015 9875 3282

Design Fireplaces
Walnut Tree Close
Guildford
Surrey GU1 4UQ
Tel: 01483 503333
Fax: 01483 570013
Email:
info@designfireplaces.co.uk
Website:
www.designfireplaces.co.uk

Dovre Castings
Unit 81
Castle Vale Industrial Estate
Minworth
Sutton Coldfield B76 8AL
Tel: 01392 474000
Email: enquiries@dovre.co.uk
Website: www.dovre.co.uk

Flames & Coal
147 Kings Road
Brentwood CM14 4EG
Tel: 01277 227043

Franco-Belge
Unit 81
Castle Vale Industrial Estate
Minworth
Sutton Coldfield B76 8AL
Email: mail@franco-belge.co.uk
Website: www.francobelge.com

Robin Gage
50 Pimlico Road
London SW1 W8LP

Gibson & Goold Ltd.
1–3 Scotland Street
Glasgow G5 8LS
Tel: 0141 429 7997
Fax: 0141 429 6606
Email:
info@scottishfireplaces.co.uk
Website:

www.scottishfireplaces.co.uk

Grate Designs
40A Camden Road
Tunbridge Wells Kent
Tel: 01892 544554
Fax: 01892 521479
Email: grate.designs@
the-internet-pages.co.uk

Harrogate Fireplaces
38–40 Kings Road
North Yorkshire HG1 5JW
Tel: 01423 565911

Heatwave
117 St Johns Hill
Sevenoaks TN13 3PE
Tel : 01732 456477

Marble Hill Fireplaces
72 Richmond Road
Twickenham
Middlesex TW1 3BE UK
Tel: 02088 921488
Fax: 02088 916591
Email: info@marblehill.co.uk
Website: www.marblehill.co.uk

Morley Stove Shop
Marsh Lane
Ware
Hertfordshire SG12 9QB
Tel: 01920 468001

Stovax Ltd.
Falcon Road
Sowton Industrial Estate
Exeter EX2 7IF
Tel: 01392 474011
Fax: 01392 219932
Email: info@stovax.com
Website: www.stovax.com

Pope Fireplaces
Unit 8
Alpha Business Park
Travellers Close
Welham Green
Hatfield
Hertfordshire AL97NT
Tel: 01707 267563

Mark Ripley Antiques & Forge
Robertsbridge
East Sussex
Tel: 01580 880324
E-mail:
Info@ripleyfireplaces.co.uk
Website:
www.ripleyfireplaces.co.uk

The Sussex Fireplace Centre
Hill House
56 Western Road
Hove
Sussex BN3 1JD
Tel: 01273 323136
Fax: 01273 721077

Thermocet UK Real Fire
Heating Centre
Telford Way
Kettering NN16 8UN

Woodford Fire of Weybridge
84 Church Street
Weybridge

Woods Fireplace Design
160–162 Oak Street
St Martins Gate
Norwich NR3 3BU

## Stained Glass

Acanthus
143 Northfields Avenue
London W13 9QR

Mark Angus
Church Road Studio
Combe Down
Bath
Avon BA2 5DL
Tel: 01225 834530

Bournemouth Stained Glass
790 Wimborne Road
Bournemouth
Dorset BH9 2DX
Tel: 01202 514734
Fax: 01202 250239

Email:
studio@stainedglass.co.uk

Susan Bradbury
Glencairn Studio
31 Fenwick Road
Kilmaurs
Kilmarnock
Ayrshire KA3 2TE
Tel/Fax: 01563 538189

Creative Glass
140d Redland Road
Bristol
Avon BS6 6YA
Tel: 0117 973 7893
Fax: 0117 923 8479
Website:
www.creative-glass.co.uk

Daedalian Glass Ltd.
The Old Smithy
Cold Row
Carr Lane
Stalmine
Poulton-le-Fylde FY6 9DW
Tel: 01253 702531
Fax: 01253 702532
Website:
www.daedalian-glass.co.uk

Glasslight Studios
The Old Pumphouse
Gloucester Place

The Maritime Quarter
Swansea SA1 1 TY

Lamplight Studio
10 Barley Mow
Passage
Chiswick
London W4 4PH

Lead & Light
35A Hartland Road
London NW1 8DB
Tel: 020 7485 0997
Fax: 020 7284 2660
Email: info @leadandlight.co.uk
Website:
www.leadandlight.co.uk

Long Eaton Stained Glass
1 Northcote Street
Long Eaton
Notts NG10 1EZ
Tel: 011 5973 2320

Prisms Glass Design
Unit 31
Kingsgate Workshops
110–116 Kingsgate Road
London NW6 2JG
Tel: 020 7624 3240
Email: prismsglass@
netscapeonline.co.uk

Paul Quail
11 Beresford Road
Holt
Norfolk NR25 6EW
Tel: 01263 71102

Sologlas Ltd.
Sologlas Technical Advisory
Service
Herald Way
Bimley
Coventry CV3 2ND
Tel: 024 7645 8021
Fax: 024 7654 7799
Website: www.solaglas.co.uk

Stained Glass
Construction & Design
62 Fairfield Street London
SW18 1DY
Tel: 020 8874 8822

Sunrise Stained Glass
58/60 Middle Street
South Street
Hants PO5 4BP
Tel: 023 9275 0512
Fax: 023 9287 5488
Email:
sunrise@stained-windows.co.uk
Website:
www.stained-windows.co.uk

Caroline Swash
88 Woodward Road
London SE22 8UT
Tel: 0208 693 6574
Fax: 0208 299 6395
Email: mswash@btinternet.com

## Bathrooms

Many architectural salvage
experts supply original
bathrooms, but it is possible
to buy good reproduction
Victorian designs made using
modern methods and easy to fit
modern plumbing.

A Touch of Brass
210 Fulham Road
London  SW10 9PJ
Tel: 0207 351 2255
Fax: 0207 352 4682
Email:
sales@atouchofbrass.co.uk
Website:
www.atouchofbrass.co.uk

Barber Wilsons & Co Ltd.
Crawley Road
London N22 6AH
Tel: 020 8888 3461
Fax: 020 8888 2041
Email: info@barwil.co.uk
Website: www.barwil.co.uk

Adamsez Ltd.
766 Upper Newtownards
Road
Dundonald BT16 1TQ
Tel: 028 9048 0465
Fax: 028 9048 0485
Email: info@adamsez.com
Website: www.adamsez.com

Heritage Bathrooms
Princess Street
Bedminster
Bristol BS3 4AG
Tel: 0117 963 3333
Email:
sales@heritagebathrooms.com
Website:
www.heritagebathrooms.com

Hill House Interiors
3 Waterloo Terrace
Baker Street
Weybridge
Surey KT13 8BS
Tel: 01932 855901
Fax: 01932 855921
Email:
shop@hillhouseinteriors.com
Website:
www.hillhouseinteriors.com

Pipe Dreams
72 Gloucester Road
London SW7 4QT
Tel: 020 7225 3978

B C Sanitan Jacuzzi UK
Silverdale Road
Newcastle-under-Lyme
Staffordshire ST5 6EL
Tel: 01782 717175
Fax: 01782 717245
Email: pr@jacuzziuk.com
Website: www.bcsanitan.co.uk

## USA

## Architectural Details & Salvage

1874 House
8070 SE 13th Avenue
Portland Oregon 97202
Tel: 503 233 1874

Architectural Salvage
Warehouse
53 Main Street
Burlington
Vermont 05401
Tel: 802 658 5011
Email: jon@greatsalvage.com
Website:
www.architecturalsalvagevt.com

Florida Victorian
Architectural Antiques
12 West Georgia Avenue
Downtown DeLand
Florida 32720
Tel: 386 734 9300
Fax: 386 734 1150
Website:
www.floridavictorian.com

Housewreckers NB & Salvage Co.
396 Somerset Street
New Brunswick
New Jersey 08901

Kayne & Son Custom
Forged Hardware
100 Daniel Ridge Road
Candler
North Caroline 28715
Tel: 828 667 8868
Fax: 828 665 8303
Website:
www.customforgedhardware.com

New Boston Building-
Wrecking Co. Inc.
135 N Beacon
Watertown MA 02172
Tel:  617 924 9090

Ohmega Salvage
2400 & 2407 San Pablo Avenue
Berkeley

California 94702
Tel: 510 204 0767
Fax: 510 843 7123
Email:
ohmegasalvage@earthlink.net
Website:
www.ohmegasalvage.com

Off the Wall Architectural
Antiques
Lincoln St. near Fifth
Box 4561
Carmel-by-the-Sea
California 93921
Tel: 831 624 6165
Website:
www.imperialearth.com

Pagliacco Turning & Milling
PO Box 225
Woodacre
California 94973
Tel: 415 488 4333
Fax: 415 488 9372
Email: pagliacco@comcast.net
Website: www.pagliacco.com

Price & Visser Millwork
2536 Valencia Street
Bellingham
Washington 98226

Red Baron's
6320 Roswell Road

Atlanta Georgia 30328
Tel: 360 734 7700

Salvage One
1840 W. Hubbard
Chicago
Illinois 60620
Tel: 312 733 0098
Fax: 312 733 6829
Website: www.salvageone.com

Second Chance
230 7th Street
Macon
Georgia 31201
Tel: 478 742 7874

Shakertown Corporation
PO Box 400
Winlock
Washington 98596
Tel: 800 426 8970

The Smoot Lumber Company
6295 Edsall Road Ste 20
Alexandria
Virginia 22312
Tel: 703  823 2100

United House Wrecking Corp
535 Hope Street
Stamford
Connecticut 06906
Urban Archaeology

137 Spring Street
New York
NY 10012
Email:
sales@urbanarchaeology.com
Website:
www.urbanarchaeology.com

## Moldings – Wood, Plaster – Door Furniture

Acorn Manufacturing Co. Inc.
457 School Road
PO Box 31
Mansfield
Massachusetts 02048
Tel: 800 835 0121
Email:
acorninfo@acornmfg.com
Website: www.acornmfg.com

Alexandria Wood Joinery
Plumer Hill Road
Alexandria
New Hampshire 03222
Tel: 603 744 8243
Fax: 603 744 3137

American Wood
Column Corporation
913 Grand Street
Brooklyn
New York NY 11211
Tel: 718 782 3163
Fax: 718 387 9099

Anglo-American Brass
Company
PO Box 9487
San Jose
California 95157
Tel: 408 246 0203
Fax: 408 248 1308
Website: http://www.aecinfo.
com/1/company/05/59/19/
company_1.html

Anthony Wood Products
PO Box 1081-S
Hilsboro
Texas 76645

Antique Hardware
509 Tangle Drive
Jamestown
North Carolina 27282
Tel: 336 454 3583

Archicast
2527 Broad Avenue
Memphis
Tennessee 38112
Tel: 901 323 8717
Email: archicast@bellsouth.net
Website: www.archicast.com

Architectural Stairbuilding &
Handrailing
15 Delaware Street
Cooperstown

New York 13326
Tel: 607 547 5863
Website: www.jamesrdean.com

Ashwood Restoration
76 New Broadway
2nd Floor North
Tarrytown
New York 10591
Tel/Fax: 914 631 9226

Baldwin Hardware Corporation
841 Wyoming Blvd
Box 15048
Reading
Pennsylvania 19612
Tel:  800 566 1986
Fax: 610 796 4601
Website:
www.baldwinhardware.com

Ball & Ball
463 W Lincoln Hwy
Exton
Pennsylvania 19341
Tel: 610 363 7330
Fax: 610 363 7639
Website:
www.ballandball-us.com

Beech River Mill Co.
Old Route
16 B Centre
Ossipee

New Hampshire 03814
Tel: 603 539 2636
Fax: 603 539 1384
Email:
beechrivermill@verizon.net
Website:
www.beechrivermill.com

Bona Decorative Hardware
3073 Madison Road
Oakley
Ohio 45209
Tel: 513 321 777
Email: bona@cinci.rr.com
Website:
www.bonahardware.com/

Breakfast Woodworks
135 Leetes Island Road
Guilford
Connecticut 06437
Tel: 203 458 8888

Carpenter & Smith Restorations
Box 504
Highland Park
Illinois 60035
Email: pnicolazzi@wi.rr.com
Website: www.saveold.com

Decorative Hardware Studio
PO Box 627
180 Hunts Lane
Chappaqua

NY 10514
Tel: 914 238 5251
Fax: 914 238 4880
Email: decordhwr@aol.com
Website:
www.decorative-hardware.com

Decorators Supply Corp
3610–12 S Morgan St rear
Chicago
Illinois 60609
Tel: 773 847 6300
Fax: 773 847 6357
Email:
info@DecoratorsSupply.com
Website:
www.decoratorssupply.com

Driwood Molding Company
PO Box 1729
Florence
South Carolina 29503
Tel: 843 669 2478
Fax: 843  669 4874
Email: sales@driwood.com
Website: www.driwood.com

Drums Sash & Door Co. Inc.
PO Box 207
Drums
Pennsylvania 18222
Tel: 570 788 1145
Fax: 570 788 3007

Email:
woodworking@intergrafix.net
Website:
www.drumssashanddoor.com

Elk Valley Woodworking Inc.
Rt 1 Box 88
Carter
Oklahoma 73627
Tel: 580 486 3337
Fax: 580 486 3491

Felber Ornamental Plastering
Corp
P.O. Box 57
1000 W. Washington Street
Norristown
PA 19404
Tel: 610 275 4713
Fax: 610 275 6636
Website: www.felber.net

C G Girolami & Sons
944 N Spaulding Avenue
Chicago
Illinois 60651
Tel: 773 227 1559

Hippo Hardware & Trading Co.
1040 E. Burnside Street
Portland OR 97214
Tel: 503 231 1444
Fax: 503-231-5708
Website: www.hippohardware.com

Hosek Manufacturing Co.
4877 National Western Drive
Denver Colorado 80216

The Joinery Co.
PO Box 518 OC8
Tarboro
North Carolina 27886
Tel: 919 823-3306

Kayne & Son Custom Forged
Hardware
100 Daniel Ridge Road
Candler
NC 28715
Tel: 828 667 8868/828 665 1988
Fax: 828 665 8303
Website:
www.customforgedhardware.com

Kenmore Industries
1 Thompson Square
PO Box 34
Boston
Massachusetts 02129

L H Freedman Studios
368 Congress St
5th Floor
Boston
Massachusetts 02210

Mad River Wood Works
PO Box 1067
Blue Lake
California 95525
Tel: 707 668 5671
Email:
info@madriverwoodworks.com
Website:
www.madriverwoodworks.com

Mangione Plaster
21 John Street
Saugerties
NY 12477
Tel: 845 247 9248

Artisans of the Valley
103 Corrine Drive
Pennington
New Jersey
Tel: 609 637 0450
Email: woodworkers@
artisansofthevalley.com
Website:
www.artisansofthevalley.com

W F Norman Corporation
214 N. Cedar
P.O. Box 323
Nevada
MO 64772
Tel: 800 641 4038/417 667 5552
Fax: 417-667-2708
Website: www.wfnorman.com

Old & Elegant Distributing
10203 Main Street Lane
City of Paris Building
Bellevue
WA 98004
Tel: 425 455 4660
Fax: 425 455 0203
Email: staff@oldandelegant.com
Website:
www.oldandelegant.com

Oregon Wooden
Screen Door Co.
330 High Street
Eugene
Oregon 97401
Tel: 541 485 0279

Pagliacco Turning & Milling
P.O. Box 229
Woodacre, CA 94973-0229
Tel: 415 488 4333
Fax: 415 488 9372
Email: pagliacco@comcast.net
Website: www.pagliacco.com

Perkins Architectural Millwork
& Hardwood Moldings
Rt 5 Box 264-W
Longview
Texas 75601
Tel: 903-663-3036

Pinecrest
2118 Blaisdell Avenue
Minneapolis
Minnesota 55404
Tel: 612 871 7071
Fax: 612 871 8956
Email: info@pinecrestinc.com
Website: www.pinecrestinc.com

Price & Visser Millwork
2536 Valencia Street
Bellingham
Washington 98226
Tel: 360 734 7700

Second Chance
230 7th Street
Macon
Georgia 31202
Tel: 478 742 7874

Silver Creek Mill
Englers Block
1335 W Hwy 76
Branson
Missouri 65616
Tel: 417 335 6645

The Smoot Lumber Company
6295 Edsall Rd Ste 20
Alexandria, VA 22312
Tel: 703 823 2100

Van Dyke Supply Company
Box 278
Woonsocket
SD 57385
Tel: 800 787 3355
Website: www.vandykes.com

Walbrook Mill &
Lumber Co. Inc.
2636 W North Avenue
Baltimore
Maryland 21216
Tel: 410 462 2200
Fax: 410 225 0212
Website:
www.walbrooklumber.com

J P Weaver Co.
911 Air Way
Glendale
California 91201
Tel: 818 500 1740
Fax: 818 500 1798
Email: info@jpweaver.com
Website: www.jpweaver.com

Williamsburg Blacksmiths Inc.
26 Williams Street
Williamsburg
MA 01096
Tel: 800 248 1776
Fax: 413 268 9317
Website:
williamsburgblacksmiths.com/

Windham Millworks
PO Box 684
Roosevelt Trail
Windham
ME 04062
Tel: 207 892 3238
Fax: 207 892 5905
Email:
info@windhammillwork.com
Website:
www.windhammillwork.com

## Sanitary Ware

A-Ball Plumbing Supply
1703 W Burnside Street
Portland
Oregon 97209
Tel: 800 228 0134
Email: aball@plumbnet.com
Website: www.a-ball.com

Antique Baths & Kitchens
2220 Carlton Way
Santa Barbara
CA 93109
Tel: 805 962 2598

Baldwin Hardware Corporation
841 Wyoming Blvd
Box 15048
Reading
Pennsylvania 19612
Fax: 610 796 4601

Email:
IntlInquiry@baldwinhq.com
Website: www.archetypes.com

Bona Decorative Hardware
3073 Madison Road
Cincinnati
Ohio 45209
Tel: 513 321 7877
Email: bona@cinci.rr.com
Website:
www.bonahardware.com

Decorative Hardware Studio
PO Box 627
180 Hunts Lane
Chappaqua
NY 10514
Tel: 914 238 5251
Fax: 914 238 4880
Email: decordhwr@aol.com
Website:
www.decorative-hardware.com

Mac the Antique Plumber
885 57th Street
OC-87
Sacramento
California 95819
Fax: 916 454 4150
Website:
www.antiqueplumber.com

Old & Elegant Distributing
10203 Main Street Lane
Dept OHJ
Bellevue
Washington 98004
Tel: 425 455 4660
Fax: 425 455 0203
Email: staff@oldandelegant.com
Website:
www.oldandelegant.com

Omnia Industries Inc.
Box 330
Cedar Grove
New Jersey 07009
Tel: 973 239 7272
Website:
www.omniaindustries.com

The Sink Factory
2140 San Pablo Avenue
Berkeley
California 94702
Tel: 510 540 8193
Website: www.sinkfactory.com

## Lighting

B & P Lamp Supply Co. Inc.
Route 3
McMinnville
Tennessee 371 10
Tel: 931 473 3016

Email: sales@bplampsupply.com
Website:
www.bplampsupply.com

The Kardell Studio Inc.
904 Westminster Street NW
Washington DC 20001
Tel: 202 462 4433

William Spencer Inc.
118 Creek Road
Rancocas Woods Village
of Shops
Mt. Laurel
NJ 08054
Tel: 856 235 1830
Email:
Info@WilliamSpencerInc.com
Website:
www.williamspencerinc.com

Yankee Craftsman
357 Commonwealth Road
Rt 30
Wayland
Massachusetts 01778
Tel: 508 653 0031
Fax: 508 650 4744
Website:
www.yankeecraftsman.com

## Glass

Backstrom Stained Glass et al
PO Box 2311
Columbus
Mississippi 39704
Tel: 662 328 7213

The Cedar Guild
51579 Gates Bridge E
Gates
Oregon 97346
Tel:  503 897 2541
Website: www.cedar-guild.com

Curran Art Glass Inc.
4520 Irving Park Road
Chicago
Illinois 60641
Tel: 708 795 8620
Fax: 708 795 9434
Website: www.curranglass.com

Golden Age Glassworks
Bellvale Road
Warwick
New York 10990
Tel: 570 729 8687
Email:
info@goldenageglassworks.com
Website:
www.goldenageglassworks.com

Great Gatsbys
5070 Peachtree Ind Blvd
Chamblee
Georgia 30341
Tel: 1 770 457 1903
Email:
internet@greatgatsbys.com
Website:
www.greatgatsbys.com/

Morgan Bockius Studios Inc.
Trumbauersville
Pennsylvania 18970
Tel: 215 672 6547

## Tiles, Marble, Stone

American Olean Tile Co.
PO Box 271
Lansdale
Pennsylvania 19446
Website:
www.americanolean.com

Designs in Tile
PO Box 4983
Dept C
Foster City
California 94404
Tel: 415 571 7122

Firebird Inc 335 Snyder Avenue
Berkeley Heights New Jersey
07922

The New England Slate Co.
1385 U S  Route 7
Pittsford
Vermont 05763
Tel: 802 247 8809
Fax: 802 247 0089
Email: slate@neslate.com
Website: www.neslate.com

New York Marble Works Inc.
1399 Park Avenue
New York
NY 10029
Tel:  212  534 2242

Penn Big Bed Slate Co. Inc.
PO Box 184
8450 Brown Street
Slatington
Pennsylvania 18080
Tel: 610 767 4601
Fax: 610 767 9252
Email: pennbbs@aol.com
Website: pennbigbedslate.com

Roman Marble Co.
120 W Kinzie
Chicago
Illinois 60610
Tel: 312 337 2217
Fax: 312 337 9865
Website:
www.romanmarble.com

Starbuck Goldner
315 W 4th Street
Bethlehem
Pennsylvania 18015
Tel: 610 866 6321
Tel: 610 866 7701
Email: info @starbucktile.com
Website: www.starbucktile.com/

Terra Designs Inc.
241 E Blackwell St
Dover
NJ 07801
Tel:  973 328 1135

United States Ceramic
Tile Company
4244 Mount Pleasant St NW
Suite 100
North Canton
Ohio 44720
Tel: 800 321 0684/330 649 5000
Fax: 330 649 5055
Email: info@usctco.com
Website: www.usctco.com

## Fireplaces

Barnstable Stove Shop
Box 472
Rt 149 Massachusetts 02668
Tel: 508-362-9913
Email: info@barnstablestove.com
Website:
www.barnstablestove.com

Brick Stove Works
374 Nelson Ridge South
Washington
Maine 04574
Tel: 207 845 2440
Fax: 207 845 2440
Email: jpmanley@midcoast.com

Bryant Stove Works
RFD 2 Box 2048
Thorndike
Maine 04986
Tel: 207 568 3665
Website: www.bryantstove.com

Homestead Chimney
PO Box 5182
Clinton
New Jersey 08809
Tel: 908 735 7708

The Reggio Register Co.
31 Jytek Road
Leominster

MA 01453
Tel: 800 880 3090
Email:
reggio@reggioregister.com
Website:
www.reggioregister.com

Saltbox
3004 Columbia Avenue
Lancaster
Pennsylvania 17603
Tel: 717 392 5649
Fax: 717 509 3127
Website:
www.americanperiod.com

Woodstock Soapstone Co. Inc.
Airpark Road
Box 37H/395
W Lebanon
New Hampshire 03784
Tel: 603 298 5955
Email: info@woodstove.com
Website:
www.woodstocksoapstone.com

## Wall finishes

Alcott & Bentley
918 Baxter Avenue
Louisville
Kentucky 40204
Tel:  502 584 8660

Bradbury & Bradbury
Wallpapers
PO Box 1 55-C
Benicia
California 94510
Tel: 707 746 1900
Fax: 707 745 9417
Email: info@bradbury.com
Website: www.bradbury.com

J R Burrows & Co.
PO Box 522
Rockland
Massachusetts 02370
Tel: 800 347 1795/781 982 1812
Fax: 781 982 1636
E-mail: merchant@burrows.com
Website: www.burrows.com

Cyrus Clark Co. Inc.
267 Fifth Avenue
New York
NY 10016
Tel: 212 684 5312
Fax: 212 481 3528
E-mail:
cyrusclark@worldnet.ntt.net
Website: www.cyrusclark.com

Katzenbach & Warren Inc.
23645 Mercantile Road
Cleveland
Ohio 44122
Tel: 216 464 3700

Raintree Designs Inc.
979 Third Avenue
New York
NY 10022

Scalamandre
37–24 24th Street
Long Island City
NY 11101
Tel: 718 361 8500
Fax: 718 361 8311
Email: info@scalamandre.com
Website:
www.scalamandre.com

F Schumacher & Co.
939 Third Avenue
New York
NY 10022
Website:
www.fschumacher.com

## Garden Furniture and Conservatories

Cassidy Bros Forge Inc.
US Route 1
Rowley
Massachusetts 01969
Tel: 978 948 7303
Fax: 978 948 7629
Email: info@cassidybros.com
Website:
http://www.cassidybros.com

Country Casual
17317 Germantown Road
Germantown
Maryland 20874
Tel: 800 284 8325

Fergusons Cut Glass Works
5890 E. Harbor Rd.
Marblehead
OH 43440
Tel: 419 734 0600

G Krug & Son Inc.
415 W. Saratoga Street
Baltimore
Maryland 21201
Tel: 410 752 3166
Fax: 410 685 6091

Park Place
2251 Wisconsin Avenue NW
Washington DC 20007
Tel: 202 342 6294

Robinson Iron Corporation
PO Box 1119
Alexander City
Alabama 35010
Tel: 256 329 8486
Fax: 256 329 8960
Email: luke@robinsoniron.com
Website:
www.robinsoniron.com

# AUSTRALIA
## Fireplaces

Amazing Grates
398 Lygon Street
Brunswick
Melbourne 3057
Tel: 03 9387 6295

Victoria Antique Firegrates
635 Canterbury Road
Surrey Hills
Melbourne
Victoria
Tel: 03 9898 5040

Antique Fireplace Restoration
77 Victoria St
Rozelle
Sydney 3127
Tel: 02 9810 6600

The Pot Belly Stove Co.
1138 Burwood Highway
Fern Tree Gully
Melbourne
Victoria 3156
Tel: 03 9758 7777
Fax: 03 9758 7961
Email: sharon@
heatingcoolingbbq.com.au
Website:
www.heatingcoolingbbq.com.au

## Glass

Astor Glass Industries
154 Hume Highway
Lansvale
NSW 2166
Tel: 02 9726 2766

Bevelite Glass Pty Ltd.
3/14 Anvil Road
Seven Hills
NSW 2147
Tel: 02 9896 0566

Castlead Works
32 Industrial Ave
Thomastown
VIC 2210 3074
Tel: 03 9359 5811

Nielsen & Moller Pty Ltd.
PO Box 289
Caringbah
NSW 2229

Oliver-Davey Glass Co.
PO Box 238
Noble Park
Victoria 3174

## Tiles

The Olde English Tile Factory
73–79 Parramatta Road
Camperdown
NSW 2050
Tel: 61 2 9519 4333
Fax: 61 2 9516 4893
Email:
tiles@oldeenglishtiles.com.au
Website:
www.oldeenglishtiles.com.au

Classic Ceramics
25 Balmain Road
Leichhardt NSW 2040
Tel: 02 9560 6555

Classic Ceramics
87–89 Queensbridge St
Southbank
VIC 3006
Tel: 03 9682 6555

Crosby Tiles
46 Hector Street
Osbourne Park
WE 6017
Tel: 9446 6000
Fax: 9446 2856
Email: sales@crosbytiles.com.au
Website: www.crosbytiles.com.au

Mingarelli Tiles Bros
90 Cochranes Road
Moorabbin
VIC 3189
Tel: 03 9555 9766

Signorino Ceramics
847 Sydney Road
Brunswick
Victoria 3056
Tel: 03 9383 1788

## FRANCE
### Ironwork/Staircases

Ets CS Schmidt
15–17 Passage de la Main d'Or
75011 Paris
Tel: 01 48 06 57 19
Fax: 01 48 06 62 22
Email:
schmidt.bronzier@wanadoo.fr
Website: charles-schmidt.fr

Sercomet SAS
28 rue Marguerite Pepier
42240 Unieux
France
Tel: 04 77 56 11 72
Fax: 04 77 56 18 69

## Conservatories

Atelier 2B
5 et 13 rue Lacharriere
75011 Paris
Tel: 01 43 38 61 40
Website: www.atelier2b.com

Poterie de la Madeleine
Tornac
30140 Anduze
Tel: 04 66 61 63 44/
06 09 51 14 61
Fax: 04 66 61 87 29

## Stoves & Fireplaces

Cheminees Philippe
Avenue Kennedy
BP 26
62400 Bethune
Tel: 03 21 61 70 70

Franco-Belge BP
59660 Merville
Tel: 03 28 43 43 43
Fax: 03 28 43 43 99

Carrieres du Boulonnais
Ferques
62250 Ferques
Website:
www.carrieresduboulonnais.fr

Gauthier Marbrerie
2–4 rue des Dremeaux
71 400 Autun
Tel: 03 85 86 57 17
Fax: 03 85 86 57 19
Website:
www.gauthier-france.com

## Fireplaces

Carrieres du Boulonnais
Ferques
62250 Ferques
Website:
www.carrieresduboulonnais.fr

Carrieres d'Etrochey
Ste-Colombe/Seine
21400 Sainte-Colombe-
sur-Seine
Tel: 03 80 91 03 38
Fax: 03 80 91 23 84
Website:
www.carrieres-etrochey.com

Gauthier Marbrerie
2–4 rue des Dremeaux
71400 Autun
Tel: 03 85 86 57 17
Fax: 03 85 86 57 19
Website:
www.gauthier-france.com

Isocheminee
93 Route Pluguffan
29000 Quimper
Tel: 02 98 55 01 04

## GERMANY
### Fireplaces

Erwin Koppe GmbH + Co
Stegenthumbacher Str. 4–6
92676 Eschenbach
Freistaat Bayern
Tel: 09645/88-0
Fax: 09645/88-40

## HOLLAND

Sol Sierhekwerk
Hurksestraat 20
5652 AK Eindhoven
Tel: 040 251 83 19
Fax: 040 255 01 91
Email: info@sol.nl

Jos Harm BY Vijzelgracht
29–31 1017 HN Amsterdam
Tel: 020 624 97 25
Fax: 020 622 63 29

# Index

# Picture Credits

# Photography